Playing the Violin

A pedagogical analysis of violin technique and performance practice

Derek J. Voigt

HARVEY WHITNEY BOOKS COMPANY
CINCINNATI, OHIO USA

Copyright © 2015 by HARVEY WHITNEY BOOKS COMPANY

All rights reserved. No part of this publication may be reproduced, distributed, or transmitted in any form or by any means, including photocopying, recording, or other electronic or mechanical methods, without the prior written permission of the publisher, except in the case of brief quotations embodied in critical reviews and certain other noncommercial uses permitted by copyright law. For permission requests or available discounts on quantity purchases, contact the publisher at the address below.

HARVEY WHITNEY BOOKS COMPANY
4906 Cooper Rd., P.O. Box 42435, Cincinnati, OH 45242 USA
Toll free: (877) 742-7631; (513) 793-3555; Fax (513) 793-3600
www.hwbooks.com

Printed in the United States of America

First Printing, 2015
Cover design by Derek J Voigt
ISBN 978-0-929375-13-7

Preface

Violin playing is a challenging, yet rewarding endeavor and profession. Success depends on individual practice, determination, motivation, and enjoyment. Though a violinist can love to play his or her instrument and create a successful and musical performance at any skill level or age, mastering violin technique and developing an understanding of the fundamentals of musicality can truly take music performance to new heights. This book provides tools and techniques to the aspiring violinist to aid in his or her quest to attain technical proficiency on the violin.

Success in violin playing stems directly from many hours of dedicated and focused practice. The industrious and dedicated students are the ones who will most prosper. The ability to play the violin is never the sole result of innate skills, but rather the direct result of a student's musical upbringing. While it's true that some children seem to born with musical talents, their skills are linked to the activities and music they were exposed to at an incredibly early age. As a result, some of the best violinists gained their talents by learning proper violin technique from the beginning of their studies. By using this book, a student who already knows the basics of violin technique will be able to tune his or her technical skills to continue down the path to technical and artistic mastery of the violin.

Not all of the ideas and exercises presented in this book have been newly created by me. Rather, many of these concepts have been around for centuries and passed down through many generations of teachers and students. Following the preface, you will find my "Pedagogy Tree." This tree outlines my primary teachers, their teachers, their teacher's teachers, and so on. Many of the names on the tree are quite famous and easily recognizable, like Ivan Galamian, Dorothy DeLay, and Arcangelo Corelli, while others are not as widely known. No matter the teacher, everyone on the tree passed valuable violinistic and musical ideas on to his or her students who, in turn, passed those ideas on to their students and, so on, until these same ideas were finally passed on to me. In writing this book, I combined the myriad ideas of the various schools of thought that contributed to my musical upbringing in an attempt to create a comprehensive pedagogical analysis of violin technique and performance practice.

This work analyzes the various motions and sensations that contribute to violin technique and provides methods to learn and master these techniques. Though this work discusses most of the techniques used in violin playing, it is not possible to discuss every aspect of violin technique in any book. Technique is incredibly personal; every musician must first understand the basics of technique before exploring more advanced methods. Building strong introductory skills will give students a strong foundation upon which to develop their own unique and sophisticated style.

This work is primarily intended for students who already understand the basics of most violin techniques and who wish, with the help of a skilled and experienced teacher, to enhance their playing ability by improving technique and musicality. This book is also suitable for advanced players and teachers who wish to improve their techniques while learning new and effective teaching strategies for almost every violinistic issue.

I would like to strongly reinforce the idea that a musical education is not a journey to be undertaken alone by any person at any age. Every student needs an experienced, disciplined, and skilled teacher to guide him or her down the correct technical and musical paths. Every bow stroke or vibrato gesture has an appropriate time and place in a piece of music and a composition can completely lose its power and influence if the wrong stroke or vibrato combination is used. The teacher's role, in addition to instructing on the correct way to execute all technical aspects on the violin, is to understand and convey traditions in phrasing, performance practice, and overall musicality in compositions. Though this book contains explanations on how to execute the various bow strokes, perform shifts with ease and accuracy, vary vibrato to attain the desired trembling effect, and delve into the mind and soul to transfer emotions to music, a teacher must help the student transfer this language into physical gestures and turn abstract ideas into tangible thoughts and feelings.

I would like to thank everyone who supported me throughout my musical upbringing, including my primary teachers, Dmitry Gerikh, Susan Waterbury, and Dr. Piotr Milewski, each of whom instilled in me not only the violinistic and pedagogical tools necessary to succeed in performance and teaching, but also a deep-rooted love for music and the violin. I would also like to thank my sister, Jessica Daviso, who edited this book. She, at a very young age, was the one who encouraged me to begin studying violin. I would also like to thank my parents for encouraging my musical education. Without their support and constant practice reminders, I would not have become the violinist and individual I am today. Finally, I would like to thank my student, Sophia Stokes, for posing for the pictures in the arm weight section of this book.

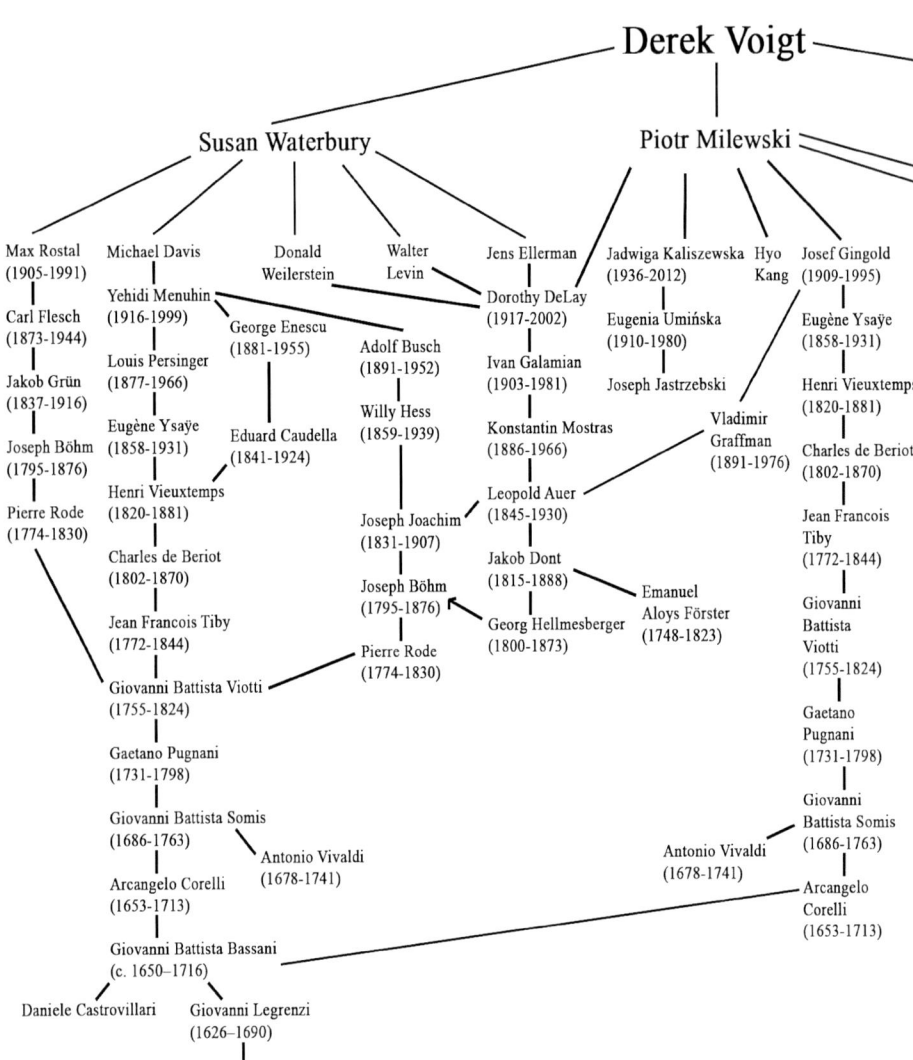

Derek Voigt

Susan Waterbury

Max Rostal
(1905-1991)

Carl Flesch
(1873-1944)

Jakob Grün
(1837-1916)

Joseph Böhm
(1795-1876)

Pierre Rode
(1774-1830)

Michael Davis

Yehidi Menuhin
(1916-1999)

Louis Persinger
(1877-1966)

Eugène Ysaÿe
(1858-1931)

Henri Vieuxtemps
(1820-1881)

Charles de Beriot
(1802-1870)

Jean Francois Tiby
(1772-1844)

Giovanni Battista Viotti
(1755-1824)

Gaetano Pugnani
(1731-1798)

Giovanni Battista Somis
(1686-1763)

Arcangelo Corelli
(1653-1713)

Giovanni Battista Bassani
(c. 1650–1716)

Daniele Castrovillari   Giovanni Legrenzi
                            (1626–1690)

                            Giovanni Maria Legrenzi

Donald
Weilerstein

George Enescu
(1881-1955)

Eduard Caudella
(1841-1924)

Walter
Levin

Adolf Busch
(1891-1952)

Willy Hess
(1859-1939)

Joseph Joachim
(1831-1907)

Joseph Böhm
(1795-1876)

Pierre Rode
(1774-1830)

Antonio Vivaldi
(1678-1741)

Piotr Milewski

Jens Ellerman

Dorothy DeLay
(1917-2002)

Ivan Galamian
(1903-1981)

Konstantin Mostras
(1886-1966)

Leopold Auer
(1845-1930)

Jakob Dont
(1815-1888)

Georg Hellmesberger
(1800-1873)

Emanuel
Aloys Förster
(1748-1823)

Jadwiga Kaliszewska   Hyo
(1936-2012)   Kang

Eugenia Umińska
(1910-1980)

Joseph Jastrzebski

Vladimir
Graffman
(1891-1976)

Antonio Vivaldi
(1678-1741)

Josef Gingold
(1909-1995)

Eugène Ysaÿe
(1858-1931)

Henri Vieuxtemps
(1820-1881)

Charles de Beriot
(1802-1870)

Jean Francois
Tiby
(1772-1844)

Giovanni
Battista
Viotti
(1755-1824)

Gaetano
Pugnani
(1731-1798)

Giovanni
Battista Somis
(1686-1763)

Arcangelo
Corelli
(1653-1713)

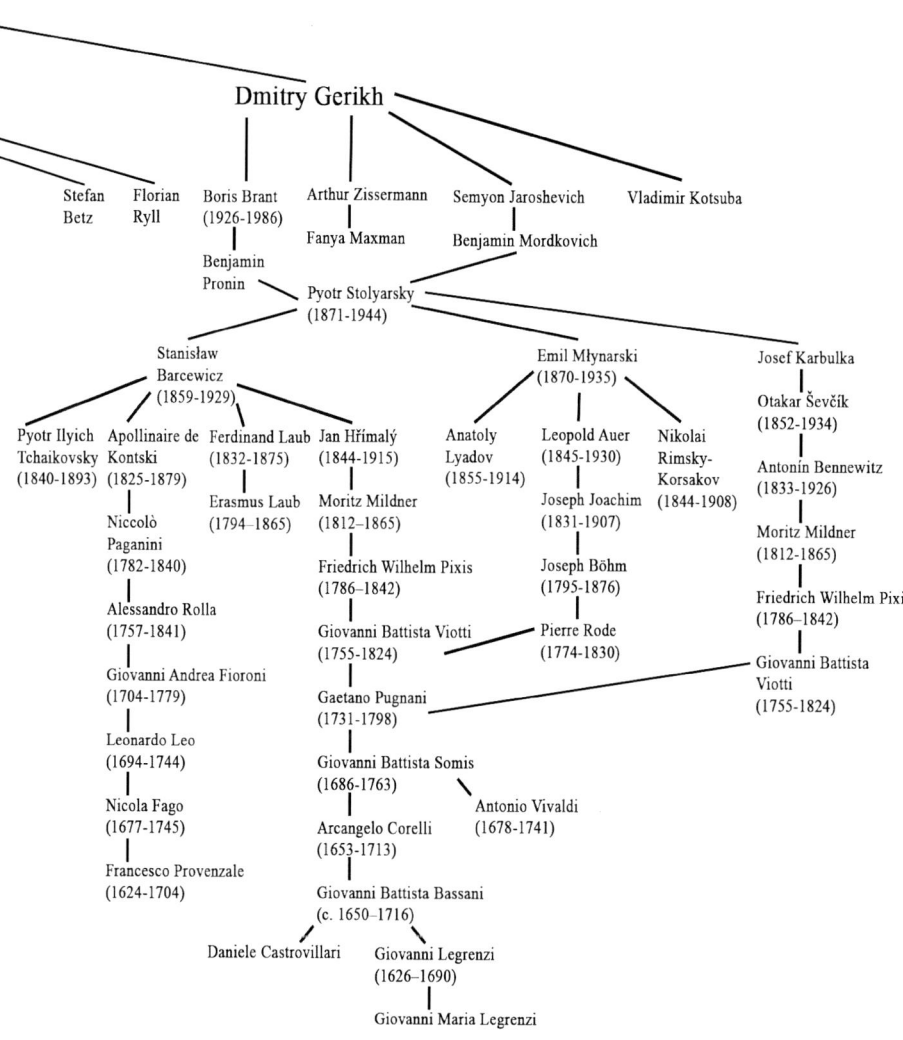

Dmitry Gerikh

Stefan
Betz

Florian
Ryll

Boris Brant
(1926-1986)

Arthur Zissermann

Semyon Jaroshevich

Vladimir Kotsuba

Benjamin
Pronin

Fanya Maxman

Benjamin Mordkovich

Pyotr Stolyarsky
(1871-1944)

Stanisław
Barcewicz
(1859-1929)

Emil Młynarski
(1870-1935)

Josef Karbulka

Pyotr Ilyich
Tchaikovsky
(1840-1893)

Apollinaire de
Kontski
(1825-1879)

Ferdinand Laub
(1832-1875)

Jan Hřímalý
(1844-1915)

Anatoly
Lyadov
(1855-1914)

Leopold Auer
(1845-1930)

Nikolai
Rimsky-
Korsakov
(1844-1908)

Otakar Ševčík
(1852-1934)

Niccolò
Paganini
(1782-1840)

Erasmus Laub
(1794–1865)

Moritz Mildner
(1812–1865)

Joseph Joachim
(1831-1907)

Antonín Bennewitz
(1833-1926)

Alessandro Rolla
(1757-1841)

Friedrich Wilhelm Pixis
(1786–1842)

Joseph Böhm
(1795-1876)

Moritz Mildner
(1812-1865)

Giovanni Andrea Fioroni
(1704-1779)

Giovanni Battista Viotti
(1755-1824)

Pierre Rode
(1774-1830)

Friedrich Wilhelm Pixis
(1786–1842)

Leonardo Leo
(1694-1744)

Gaetano Pugnani
(1731-1798)

Giovanni Battista
Viotti
(1755-1824)

Nicola Fago
(1677-1745)

Giovanni Battista Somis
(1686-1763)

Antonio Vivaldi
(1678-1741)

Francesco Provenzale
(1624-1704)

Arcangelo Corelli
(1653-1713)

Giovanni Battista Bassani
(c. 1650–1716)

Daniele Castrovillari

Giovanni Legrenzi
(1626–1690)

Giovanni Maria Legrenzi

1

The Right Hand

The right hand is arguably the most important aspect of violin technique; after all, without the right hand, no sound could be produced from the instrument. Its vital importance is the reason why I begin my book with it. It is essential to develop an excellent bow arm from the time a student first begins playing violin. Examining the right hand allows a violinist to better understand how every motion of the hand and fingers is simultaneously interconnected and separate.

As a matter of fact, the motions of the right hand affect the left hand (and vice-versa), and something as simple as posture can greatly affect bow strokes and overall comfort in the right hand. As such, if difficulties or discomforts arise in the right hand, the problem may actually come from another part of the body. For example, a student may still have difficulty playing with a straight bow while extending the right arm if the violin is too low on the shoulder. Placing the violin higher on the shoulder with the chin closer to, or even over, the tailpiece will make a straight bow path much easier to accomplish. This can be used as either a temporary or permanent solution to the problem depending on the physical build and age of the student.

An individual who has long arms may need to have the violin lower on the shoulder to attain a straight bow through an extension of the right arm, as keeping the violin high on the shoulder may inhibit some bow strokes like martelé and spiccato and may also result in a sound that lacks energy. A young student can place the violin higher on the shoulder to fix the straight bow issue, but the teacher must observe the student's development and decide whether the change should be permanent or temporary.

It is worth mentioning that all parts of this book are meant to be used as guides to violin technique. While it is comprehensive, this book is not meant to provide the only correct answer to any given issue. Violin technique is incredibly personal and a teacher must be able to determine what is correct for each student based on that individual's physical build. The techniques and recommendations I provide work well for most students, but may not be best for everyone.

Key Bow Strokes

It is essential to take a methodical approach to learning bow strokes, because understanding each step required to successfully accomplish various bow strokes will make it abundantly simpler to learn advanced techniques like spiccato, sautillé, and up-and-down-bow staccato. In this section, I break down every bow stroke to its simplest parts and explain how to execute each of them. The exercises contained at the end of the book serve as a good starting point for learning the strokes, and can be changed or adapted to suit all levels of proficiency.

Détaché

The détaché stroke is the foundation for tone on the violin. From the romantic era onward, a basic tone on the violin is a *mezzo-forte* sustained sound. All other bow strokes are a variation on this tone. To learn détaché, simply play sustained *forte* notes in the middle of the bow. Try to make all bow changes completely inaudible. This can be done in a variety of ways. First, a finger motion can be used at the tip and at the frog to start the upward motion (if preparing an up-bow) or downward motion (if preparing a down-bow) in the hand before the bow actually changes direction. The second way to make the bow changes inaudible is to slightly release the weight of the bow on the string. At the frog, the bow may come close to lifting off the string. The idea behind this method is that the string will continue to ring for the brief moment the bow releases pressure; when the bow rejoins the string, it will pick up the string's vibrations right where it left off. In the détaché stroke, the tone and dynamic need to be the same throughout the stroke. To maintain this equality, the player must exert more pressure at the tip and less pressure at the frog. When playing détaché exercises, the main focus should be tone production.

Collé

The collé stroke can be thought of as pizzicato (plucking the string) with the bow. In this stroke, the fingers are very active, while the hand and arm are largely passive. The stroke is most easily accomplished in the lower half of the bow, though it is very beneficial to practice it everywhere in the bow, as this will aid in the execution of other strokes, such as martelé and staccato. To perform the stroke, place the bow on the string in the lower half of the bow. Grab the string with the bow hair. To ensure there is enough grip, wiggle the string back and forth with the bow. Without moving the arm, pull the bow either upwards or downwards with just finger motion and lift the bow from the string. On an up-bow, the fingers start extended, with the hand slightly pronated. At the end of the stroke, the fingers will be curved. On a down-bow, the fingers will start curved, with the hand slightly supinated. At the end of the stroke, the fingers will be extended. This stroke differs from martelé in that the bow is lifted from the string. This stroke should be learned before martelé and staccato, as it is the foundation for these strokes. Also, it can be used to practice spiccato passages slowly.

Some tips:

- When grabbing the string with the bow, pull slowly to one side or the other until the string snaps back to its starting point. This will show just how much the bow is able to pull the string and will tell just how much bite is possible to achieve.
- Make the release as explosive as possible. It will give the stroke more energy, which will make the playing sound more brilliant.
- Practice collé in every part of the bow very often. This stroke is one of the best strokes for developing technique.
- To play *piano*, use a very minute finger motion. To play *forte*, use a mixture of finger motion and arm motion. However, make sure the finger motion dominates, as too much arm motion will destroy the integrity of the stroke.

Martelé

Martelé should be taught as early as possible, as learning it early on greatly facilitates learning other bow strokes and helps to develop a beautiful tone from the beginning. I like to introduce martelé as soon as an acceptable detaché is achieved. To perform this stroke, begin with the bow grabbing the string, as would be done in a collé stroke. Once the bow is grabbing the string, release the pressure while simultaneously moving the bow. Use a swift bow speed and let the bow glide across the string once the initial attack is completed. This stroke can be performed in all parts of the bow.

Some tips:

- To ensure that you have enough pressure before the stroke, wiggle the string back and forth with the bow.
- When first introducing martelé, have only the fingers perform the stroke. Use only a few inches of bow. Once this can be done, the arm may be used. Introducing martelé in this way will ensure that the fingers are utilized in the stroke.
- Practice several martelé strokes in a single bow. This will set a good foundation for staccato.

Staccato

Historically, staccato has been viewed in many different ways. Many teachers of the past, such as Leopold Auer, believed that staccato was essentially *a gift of God*, and that people either possessed the skill or did not. However, as violinists began to think of how the stroke was accomplished, they began to realize that staccato is an entirely teachable stroke. That being said, there are several different types of staccato, all of which have their own benefits and drawbacks.

The first type is by far my favorite method, as it is the most controllable, and is easily teachable to just about everyone. In this type, movement in the fingers creates the stroke. The fingers curve and straighten. At the same time, there is slight pronation and supination (see the section regarding pronation and supination for further explanations) in the hand. It can be thought of as a series of very quick and controlled martelé strokes. To perform staccato in this way, it is useful to hold the bow lightly with just the index finger, ring finger, and the thumb. Put the bow on the string as in a collé stroke. Without moving the arm, wrist, or hand, push the bow either upwards or downwards with just finger motion. If doing an up-bow staccato, make sure the fingers start extended and the hand is slightly pronated. At the end of the stroke, the fingers will be curved. If doing a down-bow staccato, the fingers will start curved, with the hand slightly supinated. At the end of the stroke, the fingers will be extended. It is important to mention that in this type of staccato, the forearm and upper arm remain passive. First practice about 10 slow notes per bow, and then gradually increase the number of notes per bow and the speed of the notes.

In the second type of staccato, the impulse comes from the forearm. The fingers should still be flexible, but do not generate the stroke, as in the first type. The upper arm also remains passive. This type is also relatively-controllable. It should be practiced in the same manner as the first type.

In the third type of staccato, the entire arm remains stiff, and the impulse is generated in the upper arm. In many cases, this impulse feels like the arm is twitching. For many people, this type of staccato is not controllable, which is why I personally do not like it. This type of staccato, when mastered, sounds brilliant and can be played at amazingly high speeds.

Some tips:

Up-Bow Staccato
- Play on the outer edge of the hair
- Play with a slightly elevated elbow
- Angle the point of the bow slightly toward the fingerboard
- Lean on the hand slightly towards the fourth finger

Down-Bow Staccato
- Play on the inner edge of the hair
- Play with a slightly lower elbow
- Angle the point of the bow slightly towards the bridge
- Lean the hand onto the first finger

Flying Staccato

Many historical violinists, like Pablo de Sarasate, used only this type of staccato. It consists of a series of lifted staccato strokes in one bow. This stroke can be played in all parts of the bow. At the frog, the stroke will be relatively short, forte, and with a big sound. In the middle, the stroke will be short, piano, and graceful. At the tip, the stroke will be very short, pianissimo, and almost sneaky. To execute this stroke, perform the first type of staccato stroke described above, but lift the bow after each iteration of the stroke.

This type of staccato is most often used in passages that consist of runs that start on the string, but end off the string. A great example of this is found in Paganini's 13th Caprice.

The first several descending thirds are often played on the string with a portato or staccato stroke, but the remaining ones are most often played with the flying staccato stroke.

Spiccato

This bouncing stroke is essential to almost all violin repertoire and mastery of this technique is paramount. As such, I highly recommend teaching spiccato as early as possible. Spiccato can be played in various parts of the bow, from the frog to the middle, to attain various colors and effects. A spiccato at the frog produces long and heavy tones, whereas a spiccato in the middle produces much shorter and lighter tones. To begin a spiccato stroke, the following steps can be used. First, start the bow bouncing in the middle of the bow. No sound will be produced. Make sure neither the arm nor hand moves. The bounce is generated by a combination of dropping the bow on the string, letting it rebound and continue to bounce naturally, and gently nudging the bow downward with the index finger to control the bounce height and number of bounces. Next, using the fingertips and slightly the hand, add length to the bow strokes just barely until you can hear a pitch. The notes will be very short, and the tone will most likely be harsh. Practice this stroke until the notes ring and the tone is clear. When practicing this bow stroke in the context of a piece, do not just begin the section, but rather, play 10-20 repeated notes on the first pitch until you attain a clear and ringing tone before proceeding to the rest of the notes.

Ricochet

There are two main ways to approach the ricochet stroke. In the first method, the bow is thrown onto the string by the first finger and allowed to bounce a prescribed number of times. To accomplish this, loosen all the fingers of the hand and gently nudge the bow toward the string using the first finger. The thumb will act as a fulcrum, with the fingers and the wood of the bow moving around it. The bow will bounce off the string on its own. How hard the bow is thrown onto the string will determine how loud the stroke will be, how high the bow will rebound, and how fast the bow will bounce. The harder the bow is thrown, the higher it will rebound, the louder the stroke will be, and the slower the bounce will be. The length of bow used is proportional to the number of notes played.

In the second method, the wrist is swiftly thrown downwards, which results in a bouncing bow. To accomplish this, hold the bow incredibly lightly just above the balance point and throw down the wrist swiftly and with a lot of force. The bow will bounce very high the first few times then the bounces will become increasingly lower and faster until the bow ceases to bounce. The height of the bounce and its volume will be determined by how hard the wrist is thrown downwards. The harder the wrist is thrown, the higher the bounce and the louder the volume. When first learning this type, it is helpful to only hold the stick with the second finger and the thumb. When playing arpeggio-ricochet, each new bow will have a new impulse in the right hand. An up-bow will be generated simply by changing the direction of the bow, rather than by creating a new impulse.

Both types of ricochet share the same general principles. Near the tip of the bow, the bounce will be faster, lower, and lighter, and will require less bow to achieve. Near the middle, the bounce will be slower, higher, and heavier, and will require more bow to achieve. The less bow that is used, the lower and faster the bounce will be, and vice-versa. Finally, it may help to slightly turn the stick of the bow towards the fingerboard, so the full hair does not contact the string. If the full hair contacts the string, the bounce may be too high, and the tone may not be as clear as if the bow was slightly tilted.

Sautillé

The sautillé stroke is unique among the bow strokes in that while the bow appears to be bouncing, the hair never actually leaves the string. To produce this stroke, simply start with a détaché stroke in the middle of the bow. Gradually use less and less bow until the stick of the bow begins to naturally bounce. The stroke will be most effective if the bow is moved by the wrist, hand, or fingers rather than the arm. Make sure the hand and fingers are very relaxed. If there is any amount of tension, the stroke will not be achieved.

Once the stroke is learned, practice a spiccato stroke on a single note, gradually increasing the tempo. Notice the tempo at which the stroke becomes a sautillé stroke. Practice both strokes at this tempo to increase proficiency. Many people find that they can perform neither stroke very well at this tempo, as the spiccato is too fast and the sautillé is too slow.

Some Tips:

- Use flat hair. The bow bounces best when the hair is flat. The flat hair will also help to produce a full tone.
- Do not try to bounce the bow.
- Pronate the hand
- This stroke is quite easy to achieve, as the bow does almost all the work. Don't try too hard to make the stroke work. Rather, just play a short and quick détaché and allow the bow to produce the stroke.

Mastering these bow strokes is essential to every violinist. Most of the strokes can be practiced while playing scales or virtually any étude or study. Use various rhythms when practicing to ensure proficiency. Also, several different strokes may be practiced at the same time. For example, a détaché and martelé can be practiced together by alternating two détaché notes and two martelé notes. I recommend playing Otakar Ševčík's Op. 3. This work is essentially an intense workout for the right hand, as it provides the violinist with many different situations in which all of the basic bow strokes can be utilized. Giuseppe Tartini's "The Art of Bowing" is another valuable resource for any violinist who wishes to enhance right-hand technique.

Tone Production

Tone gives a unique identity to each violinist; it is most often what the audience remembers about any given performance. As such, it is very important to devote a large amount of time to developing a pleasing, beautiful tone. Many variables influence a violinist's tone and changing one of them, even slightly, will often produce a drastically different sound. For this reason, it is important to know the variables at play in tone production are and how to alter them for artistic gain. As with almost every other aspect of violin playing, there are no concrete rules to tone production. Rather, the suggestions I offer should be taken with a grain (or fistful) of salt. It is important to experiment with the variables involved with tone, including weight, speed, and contact point, in order to attain the best combination for your own desired tone or effect.

Weight/Pressure

Weight or pressure can be added by various parts of the right hand or arm to attain various tones. Essentially, weight/pressure comes from a combination of arm weight, wrist level, and first finger weight (pressure). When experimenting with different combinations, it is useful to try only one variable at a time, or else it may be difficult to know which one really changed the result.

Arm Weight

Arm weight is incredibly important to generating a wonderful tone, and it is essential to incorporate it into the right arm technique. To ensure that the tremendous weight of the arm is being transferred into the string, perform the following exercise with a partner.

First Weight Transfer Point – Elbow

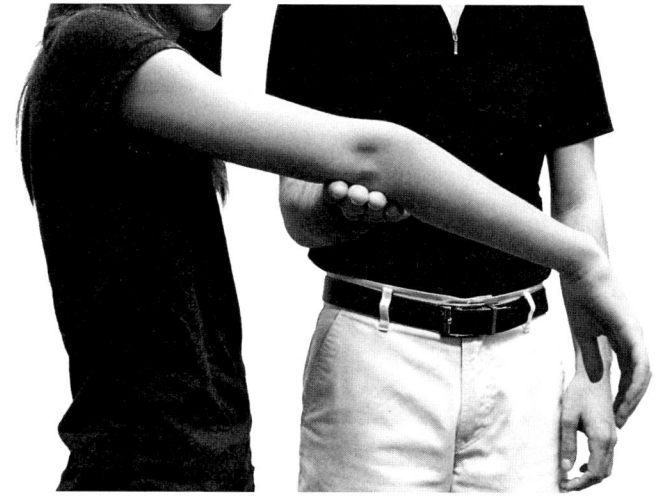

Weight Transfer Point Along Forearm

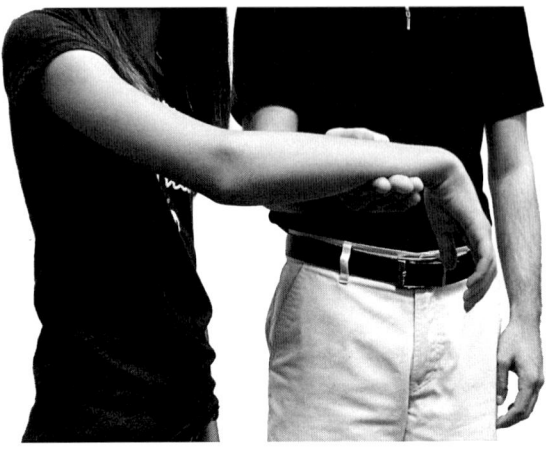

Final Weight Transfer Point – Fingers

Step 1: Place your right elbow into the palm of your partner and relax the arm, transferring all the weight into their hand.

Step 2: Using alternating hands, your partner should slowly, and incrementally, transfer the arm weight to several points along the forearm, to the wrist, and finally into the fingers. At this point, the entire arm dangles from the fingertips, which hold on to the partner's hand (preferably only one or two fingers on the partner's hand – not the whole hand).

- It is important for your partner to completely let go of your hand/arm a few times and re-start the exercise to ensure that your right arm is fully relaxed. If it is relaxed, your arm will flop lifelessly to your side. If it is not relaxed, your hand or arm will still be slightly suspended in the air, and will not flop down.

- The relaxed arm weight generated in this exercise should be transferred to the string when holding the violin. The final weight transfer point mentioned above (the fingertips) replicates the arm weight used while holding playing on the violin.

- Immediately after doing this exercise, place the bow deep in the G-String at the frog and allow the arm to hang lifelessly from it. When practicing arm weight, try to re-create this sensation.

The largest, most robust tones can be attained with arm weight. In this, the upper arm is lowered (the elbow will also be lower). This will result in the weight of the upper arm being transferred into the string. At first, it may be difficult to implement this type of weight transfer, as the feeling may be quite alien to some individuals. Arm weight should not always be the same when playing. Vary it to attain a wide variety of tonal colors.

Weight or pressure can also be added by the wrist. The higher the wrist level, the less weight will be in the string. The lower the wrist level, the more weight will be in the string. Do not push the bow in the string using the wrist. Rather, simply having a low wrist level will provide sufficient weight. Also, take care to not exaggerate a low wrist. It could result in pain or long-term medical issues.

Finally, weight or pressure can be added with the first finger. This weight can be added in a few different ways. First, it can be added with pronation of the right hand. Tilting the hand so that it leans toward the first finger, or pronation, will automatically push more weight into the string. Supinating the hand, or tilting the hand so that the knuckles are more parallel to the stick, or so the line of the hand is even tilting away from the first finger, will take weight out of the string. This technique falls between the categories of wrist and finger pressure, as the action originates in the wrist, but is felt most in the finger. Finger pressure can also be added by simply nudging the first finger into the stick; this is arguably the easiest way to add weight into the string in a controlled way. The more the first finger pushes, the greater the weight in the string.

These methods for adding weight or pressure into the string should be practiced individually to attain the most control of the right hand and arm as possible. It is important to remember that weight and pressure cannot be added without slightly altering other parts of right-hand technique, such as contact point, bow speed, or even which part of the bow is used.

Weight and Bow Speed

When weight or pressure changes, it is important to also change bow speed. As a general rule, as weight increases, bow speed should decrease. If bow speed stays constant, the volume of the sound will increase. This being said, if bow speed is increased and weight is decreased, the tone may become lighter, even airy. If a stronger, denser tone is desired, it may be desirable to keep a constant weight by altering contact point, rather than speed. Experiment with all combinations of weight and speed to understand what types of tones and effects are possible.

Contact Point

There are five general contact points on which the bow can play, ranging from very close to the bridge to very close to the fingerboard. The bow can even play completely over the fingerboard or almost on top of the bridge. However, these points are used mainly for special effects, like *sul pont*, and will not be used in normal tone production. Understanding when to play on each contact point is important not only to tone color and character, but also is a very basic principle to simple tone production.

This diagram illustrates the five basic contact points on the violin. Contact point 1 is the closest to the bridge, and contact point 5 is closest to the fingerboard. The other points fill the space between these two locations in relatively equal increments. Changes in bow speed, weight or pressure, different string level, and desired tone color all call for variation to contact point.

Sul Ponticello (Sul Pont)

If the bow contacts the string below contact point 1 (even closer towards the bridge), shrieking, whistling, and eerie sounds will be produced. This effect is achievable with many different combinations of bow weight and speed, though the resulting tones will be different depending on which combination is used. I personally prefer to use a fast bow speed combined with very little weight. The resulting sound is especially eerie, lacking core to the tone and speaking ghastly whispers. Though the tone is unpleasant for most repertoire, *Sul Pont* can be used as a special effect. It was widely used by composers in romantic and modern eras like Hector Berlioz and Eugène Ysaÿe.

Different String Levels and Contact Point

As explained in the section entitled "Pivoting and String Crossing," there are 7 different string levels. Changing between these levels requires a change in contact point to attain the same type of sound.   On the G-String, the bow should, generally-speaking, be on or between contact points 4 or 5. Playing here is necessary due to the thickness of the string. If the first or second contact points are used, the bow may not be able to sufficiently grab the string, and the resulting sound will be light, whistling, lacking depth, or even sul-pont.   Take care not to move past contact point 5. Playing over the fingerboard may result in a choked-tone, or even a wolf-tone. As you move to the D, A, and E-Strings, the contact point should move closer and closer to the bridge, until on the E-String, when it is at points 2 and 1.

Bow Speed, Dynamics, and Contact Point

Bow speed is a very important part of tone production. Not only does it affect the quality of the sound, but it also allows for different musical personalities. We've all heard violinists perform who play everything *technically* correct: in tune, in rhythm, and acceptable musicality, though the performance isn't nearly as riveting as it could be. This is often because they use too slow a bow speed. Violinists who are able to use a swift bow speed, but are able to use a very small amount of bow, have extremely exciting and high-energy performances. As I mentioned at the beginning of the chapter, it's important to take this rule with at least a grain of salt. If a violinist uses fast bow speed all the time, in an attempt to bring energy to his/her performance, there will be no variance to the tone or energy, and the audience will become exhausted and distracted rather quickly.

Contact point may be modified when altering dynamics to attain the desired tone and character at any given dynamic level. If bow speed decreases, the bow should move toward the bridge. As this change takes place, it may also be necessary to increase weight to avoid a shrill sound. If the bow moves incredibly slowly at the bridge with a fair amount of weight, a *son filé* sound will be created. It is incredibly important to practice this bow stroke extensively, as it helps train the muscles in the hand to automatically generate a pleasing tone. When playing a ***forte*** sound, the contact point will often move closer to the bridge. This combination will generate an incisive, dense, and bright sound.

Conversely, as bow speed increases, the bow should move away from the bridge toward the higher contact points. If the bow is too close to the bridge, the tone will become shrill and lose the lower overtones. This results in an unsettling feeling, and if exaggerated, may even produce harmonics or a whistling sound. However, when playing a ***piano*** sound, the contact point may move closer to, or even over, the fingerboard. Along with a ***piano*** sound, this combination will generate a loose, delicate, pale sound. Often when playing chords, the bow will need to be on contact points 4, 5, or even over the fingerboard, even when playing ***forte***. If a lower contact point is used, the tone may very well be weak, shrill, unsettling, and lack any core. It is important to practice the altering of contact points with respect to dynamics, as the tone quality may suffer if the bow is placed too close to the bridge or too close to the fingerboard.

Pivoting and String Crossing

Arm Height

As a general rule, the arm should be in a straight line with the bow. If you held your violin in front of a mirror with the scroll of the violin perpendicular to the mirrored surface, the bow and arm should form a straight line. It is okay if the arm level is slightly lower than the bow-level. If the arm level is higher than the bow-level, arm weight will not be transferred into the string. Rather, weight will be forced into the string by the entire arm. This will result in an incredibly unpleasant and tense sound. As such, it is important to alter arm height to match the level of the bow on the string.

String Levels

There are seven different levels the bow will assume. They are: (1) G-String, (2) G-D Double Stop, (3) D-String, (4) D-A Double Stop, (5) A-String, (6) A-E Double Stop, and (7) E-String. Pivoting is the movement that takes us from one level to another. This action consists of changing the arm, wrist, or hand's position from what is required for the old level to what is required for the new level. Before examining what is involved with changing levels, we must establish what position of the arm is appropriate for each. Point the scroll towards a mirror. This will allow you to properly see the levels of the upper and lower arm. The right shoulder should be completely relaxed. If it is raised, most of the right hand technique will suffer, and none of the bow strokes will be acceptably performed. As a general rule, the upper arm will be lower than the forearm. Make sure the upper arm is not higher than the forearm on the E and A-Strings. The forearm should be roughly parallel to the stick of the bow. Keeping it parallel will allow the bow to feel like an extension of the body, rather than an awkward piece of wood, and will also help produce the best possible tone. When practicing pivoting, constantly look in the mirror to confirm that these guidelines are being followed.

What initiates the string crossing? Depending on where you start and where you are going, either the hand or the elbow initiates (or leads) the motion. If going from a lower to a higher string, initiate the motion with the elbow and allow the hand to follow. If going from a higher to a lower string, initiate the motion with the hand and allow the elbow to follow. These motions are very minute, and should not be exaggerated. However, since they are very important to technique, care should be taken to ensure that they are happening.   To practice this, simply pick a piece or étude that has many string crossings or jumps from the G to E-string and play very slowly, focusing on the elbow and hand motions. Over the course of a few weeks, gradually increase the tempo. Don't play too fast too soon, or the motion will not become natural. If a piece requires a string crossing from a high string to a low string for only a few notes, especially in a fast section, it may not be necessary to change the position of the entire hand and arm. Rather, the crossing can be done with the wrist. Crossing this way will make it much easier to play fast passages where there may sporadic leaps.

In order to practice tone with regards to string crossing, start by playing with a beautiful tone on the initial string. Rather than crossing to the final string, pivot to the double stop between the two strings. Once the transition between the single note and the double stop is smooth, and a beautiful tone is attained on both levels, practice the transition between the double stop and the final string. If the initial string and final string are not adjacent to each other (if there is another string between them – i.e. Between G and A is D, and between D and E is A), it is beneficial to practice transitioning between all string levels between the initial string and the final string. The final goal of this exercise is to play the string crossing adeptly in tempo while maintaining a beautiful tone.

It is important to note that the seven levels are largely meant for theoretical analysis of technique, and in reality, there may be more levels, which are not easily definable. For example, when playing a piece of music that has many string crossings back and forth to and from adjacent strings, the bow will not be entirely on the levels of the individual strings, but rather will stay around the level of the double-stop between these strings. The wrist or even fingers will perform the string crossings. Doing this will prevent excess motion and will make the crossings sound much smoother.

Breaking Chords

There are several different ways to break chords on the violin. Each way produces a very different effect. As such, the performer needs to determine what he or she feels is best in the context of the piece of music.

Four-Note Chords

1. 2 notes plus 2 notes: Playing the bottom two strings followed by the top two strings is the most traditional way to break chords on the violin. In Romantic and Modern music, the emphasis usually lies on the upper two notes. However, in Classical, Baroque, and earlier music, the emphasis usually lies on the bottom two notes. No matter where the emphasis lies, use a very small amount of bow on the bottom two notes. You may use as much of the remaining bow for the top notes as necessary to achieve the desired effect. Performing chords with this type of bow distribution allows the performer to control every aspect of the bow, dynamics, any accents, and tone. If too much bow is used on the bottom notes, the top notes will sound forced, choked, and they will be too weak. It is also possible they will not be heard at all by the listener.

2. 1 note plus 3 notes: Playing the bottom string followed by the top three strings together is another commonly used method for breaking chords. It originated in the Russian tradition of violin playing, and works best in Romantic and Modern repertoire. It is mainly used when the performer wants to have a huge emphasis on the bass note of a chord, or when there is a series of chords in which the lowest notes contain the melody. When playing the three top strings simultaneously, the bow must have flat hair, must be slightly nearer to the fingerboard than normal, and must be on the A-String level, almost leaning toward the D-String. If the bow leans toward the E-string, the D-String may not be heard at all, and the E-String may overpower

the chord. It is very useful to practice open strings before adding the notes of the chord.

3. 3 notes plus 1 note: Playing the bottom three strings together, then playing the top string alone is sometimes used in performance, but is not as common as the first two methods. Like the second method, this one is mainly used when voice-leading is an issue in a passage. If the soprano line of a passage of chords contains the melody, a violinist may choose to break chords in this way. However, it is important to mention that a violinist may also choose the 2-Plus-2 method and simply hold out the top note if the 3-Plus-1 method is cumbersome.

4. 2 notes plus 2 notes, followed by a sustained note of the same chord: In this method, the player breaks the chord with the 2-Plus-2 method, but then sustains one of the notes of the chord. Violinists such as Heifetz, Oistrakh, and others from the Russian tradition, typically use this method when playing pieces by Bach, or other pieces that require voice leading. It is important to mention that the emphasis lies on the sustained note, not the top two notes. To perform this method, simply play the bottom two notes with very little bow, followed by the top two notes with little bow, then quickly emphasize and sustain the featured melodic note. Many early music scholars dislike the use of this method of breaking chords when playing early repertoire, like Bach, since chords were not traditionally played this way in Bach's time.

5. Playing all four notes simultaneously: This method of breaking chords is very powerful and is not found widely in

music performance. To perform this type of chord, the bow hair must be flat, the level of the bow must be on the D-A Double Stop, and the bow must be over the end of the fingerboard, if not over the fingerboard itself. Many violinists cannot play this type of chord at all due to the height or curve of their bridge. To play this type of chord, the bridge cannot be too high or too curved. The curve must be relatively flat to allow for the bow to actually play all four strings together. Most often when violinists try to play this type of chord, they are really playing only 3 of the four notes simultaneously, briefly touch one of the strings so that it resonates with the chord, or even rely on the sympathetic vibration of one of the strings.

6. Rolling a Chord (1 plus 1 plus 1 plus 1): This method is often used in all types of music. It provides the ability to create many various colors in the musical palate. Rolling a chord quickly creates one effect, while rolling it slowly creates another. At the same time, emphasizing the bottom note generates a very different sound than emphasizing the top note. It is not advisable to roll too many chords in succession, as they will stop sounding like chords and begin to sound like arpeggios. This method of breaking chords is widely accepted by scholars and musicians of all types of repertoire. It is often used in early music, as well as romantic and modern music. As such, it is probably the most versatile type of breaking chords, but do not over-use it. It creates a very special effect and should not be used to break many chords in a piece, unless the resulting sound is specifically desired.

Three-Note Chords

The methods of breaking three-note chords are essentially the same as four-note chords. For example, one method would be 2 notes plus 2 notes. Just as in 4-note chords, the 2-Plus-2 method is the most common way to break chords. To perform this type of chord, simply play the bottom two notes simultaneously, then pivot to play the top two notes simultaneously. Three note chords share the same stylistic performance guidelines as four note chords. In Romantic and Modern music, the emphasis usually lies on the upper two notes. However, in Classical, Baroque, and earlier music, the emphasis usually lies on the bottom two notes. No matter where the emphasis lies, use only a very small amount of bow on the lower notes. Three-note chords may also be broken with 1 note plus 2 notes, 2 notes plus 1 note, all together, or arpeggiated (rolling the chord). The methods for breaking chords these ways are the same as those found in the Four-Note Chord section above.

Tone Production

To generate a sweet, spinning, luscious, singing, and meaty tone, it is important to experiment with many different variables. However, sometimes it's not easy, or advisable, to simply experiment and hope for good results. After spending much time and effort developing a pleasing tone myself, I realized that developing tone is a slow process that involves training individual fingers to perform unique roles.

Roles of the Right Hand Fingers

-   Thumb: The thumb acts as a fulcrum, balancing between the pinky and the first finger. It should always be bent towards the palm and should always remain flexible in order to prevent tension and allow for different bow strokes.

-   First/Index Finger: The first finger leans into the stick in order to provide a large, deep, and meaty sound. The first finger should provide the most weight at the tip of the bow, and the least weight at the frog, in order to provide an equal sound in all parts of the bow. To practice varying necessary amounts of weight, play whole bows while performing the following exercise. At the frog, the first finger will be lifted off the stick, as to avoid any amount of weight being transferred into the stick. At the tip, the finger will be very heavy, pushing rather strongly into the stick. Though the first finger will be pushing into the bow, be sure there is no tension in the bow hand. When performing this exercise, use a *son filé* bow stroke.

-   Second/Middle Finger: The second finger, for most people, sits opposite the thumb. Its main job is to hold the bow. The second finger, like the rest of the hand, should always be loose and flexible.

-   Third/Ring Finger: The third finger is possibly the most important finger of the right hand. Unlike the other fingers, which perform technical roles, the Third Finger is an artistic finger. Its main job is to generate a pleasing tone. It accomplishes this by gently pulling in on the frog. It is most useful when only the pad of the finger is touching the frog (the finger does not hang over further than the first knuckle joint). Since this finger performs a pulling motion, it is very important to ensure that it is free of tension.

- Fourth Finger/Pinky: The fourth finger counteracts the first finger. Since the first finger is most active at the tip of the bow, the pinky will be least active at the tip. Some of the greatest violinists throughout history even lifted the pinky slightly off the bow at the tip. Since the first finger will be the most passive at the frog, the pinky will be the most active here. However, since the pinky is not a very strong finger, do not actively try to do anything with it. Don't try to force the pinky to do anything, as this will cause tension and an imbalance among the rest of the fingers. Instead, simply allow it to curve and straighten naturally as the hand supinates and pronates, respectively.

Pronation and Supination

Pronation and supination refer to the angle of the base knuckles of the right hand with respect to the bow stick. When the hand is pronated, the base knuckle of the first finger will be lower than the base knuckle of the fourth finger, which will be elevated. Conversely, when the hand is supinated, the base knuckles of the first and fourth fingers will be roughly in line with each other. The following images show pronation and supination.

Front View of Pronation

Rear View of Pronation

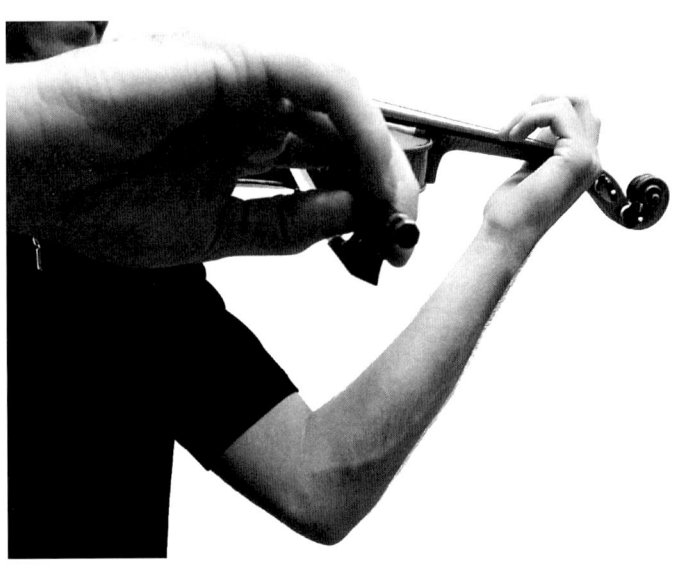

Front View of Supination

Rear View of Supination

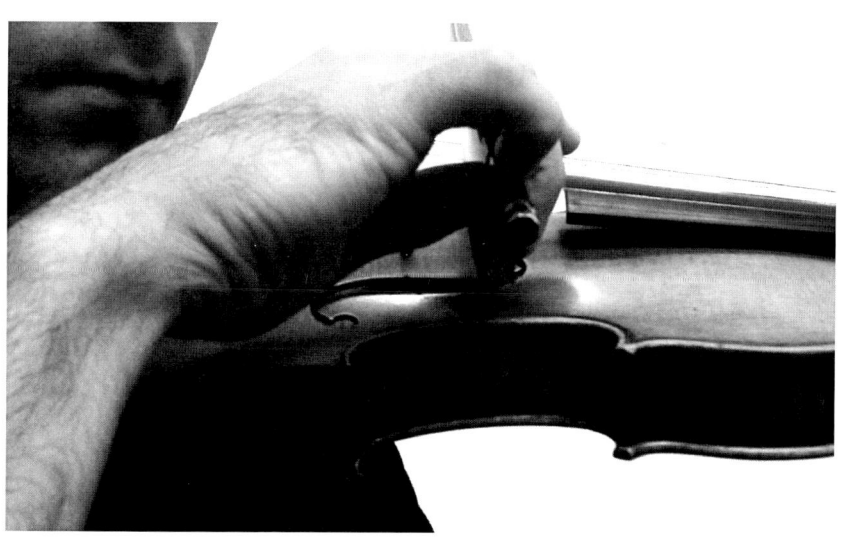

When the hand is pronated or supinated, the bow hold will appear slightly different than normal. When pronated, the bow hold will seem almost normal. Some violinists' bow holds are slightly pronated to begin with, so the pronated hold will not seem very different than the normal hold. When the hand is supinated, however, the hold will appear slightly different than normal. Since the base knuckles of all the fingers are almost at the same level, the hand will seem flat, the pinky will seem very rounded (and it will feel like the pinky is doing a lot of work), and the first finger may even become relatively straight (it may not hang over the bow stick like normal).

How to Pronate and Supinate

Even though the most noticeable changes occur within the fingers and knuckles when pronation or supination takes place, the wrist is most commonly used to pronate or supinate the hand. To pronate the hand, simply rotate the hand at the wrist (notice that the entire forearm really moves when the wrist is rotated) in a counter-clockwise direction. To supinate the hand, rotate the hand at the wrist in a clockwise direction. The rotation is very subtle, and should not be exaggerated, as to avoid tension and poor technique.

Pronation and supination, though less commonly, is accomplished only by altering knuckle height. To pronate this way, slightly straighten the pinky and make its base knuckle is wholly visible. To supinate this way, round the pinky as much as possible and make its base knuckle disappear under the skin.

When to Pronate and Supinate

There are no clear-cut rules regarding when, and how much, to pronate or supinate the hand. Rather, try pronating or supinating more or less to determine what is best for a given passage. Generally speaking, the hand should be pronated when in the upper-half of the bow and supinated when approaching the frog. This is necessary because pronation automatically adds weight into the string. This is convenient, as less finger weight/pressure will be necessary to achieve the same sound, but requires concentration on the part of the violinist to ensure that the sound is not excessive when approaching the frog. Practice the exercise provided in the above section that discusses the roles of the fingers. In this exercise, the first and fourth fingers are lifted off the bow at certain times. At the frog, the first finger will be lifted off the stick, as to avoid any amount of weight being transferred into the stick. The hand will be supinated at this point. Make sure the pinky is very round, and that the base knuckles are almost level. At the tip, the first finger will be very heavy, pushing rather strongly into the stick. Though the first finger will be pushing into the bow, be sure there is no tension in the bow hand. The hand will be pronated when at the tip. The pinky will be less rounded (for some people it may be close to straight), and the base knuckle of the pinky will be much higher than the base knuckle of the first finger. As with the exercise in the previous section, use a *son filé* bow stroke when performing this exercise.

Psychological Aspects of Tone Production

Tone production is influenced just as strongly by our thoughts as our physical actions. Focusing on tone mentally may be more beneficial than changing something physically. However, as strong as the mind is, the physical motions involved in tone production must be solidified before the psychological side of tone production is tackled. Do not try to think about too many things at once. It will be overwhelming and may have adverse results.

1. Third Finger
   - Imagine the third finger's tip is gently pulling in on the frog

2. Wrist
   - Imagine the wrist coaxes the sound out of the strings by slightly pushing into the string and to the right on down-bows and to the left on up-bows.

3. Corresponding Fingers
   - When playing, imagine that each finger is more active when its corresponding finger of the left hand is being used to play a note. For example, when the second finger is being used in the left hand, the second finger will be more active in the right hand. The sensation could also just consist of shifting attention to the finger to ensure that it is doing its role (see section above on Roles of the Fingers). To get used to this exercise, the sensation of 'activity' may be substituted by physically pulling in on the frog.

4. Vibrating Bow
   - Unknown to most violinists, the wood of the bow vibrates, just as the violin does. Try to feel the bow vibrating as you play beautiful passages. Doing this requires a relaxed bow hold and concentration.

5. Banana
   - Imagine that the path of the bow from tip to frog is in the shape of a banana – curved. At the frog, the bow will be slightly more vertical (the tip will point towards the ceiling), and at the tip, the bow will be slightly more horizontal.

6. Spinning
   - When vibrating, the strings on the violin move in a circular pattern. This can actually be observed when playing *forte* on the G-String. While playing, imagine that as the bow moves across the strings, they resonate in a circular, spinning pattern.

7. Talons
   - The hairs on the bow contain microscopic 'talons,' which grab onto the string and cause it to vibrate. While playing, imagine millions of these talons grabbing the string.

8. Sound Goes Up
   - Imagine that the bow is pulling the sound up and out of the violin. The sound is being projected upwards, rather than sideways.

9. Think of a Beautiful Sound
   - Sometimes, it is easiest to just think of playing with the most beautiful sound imaginable.

These suggestions may seem inconsequential, but they actually make a huge difference in tone. As I mentioned earlier, do not try to think about more than one thing at a time. Doing so will reduce the amount of success, and may actually produce a worse tone than thinking about nothing at all.

Right Hand Technique, with all its nuances, is always a work in progress. Even when the bow strokes are performed expertly, tone is clear, projective, ringing, and gorgeous, and musicality is evident, everything can be better in some way.

When practicing, devote at least 1 hour to perfecting bow strokes. While doing this, always concentrate on having a clear and pleasing tone, and think about some aspect of right-arm technique. Books like Otakar Ševčík's *40 Variations,* Op. 3, or Giuseppe Tartini's *The Art of Bowing*, contain excellent exercises that can be used to improve right-hand technique. Each work is a piece in a theme and variations form. Each variation uses a combination of different bow strokes, amounts of bow, dynamics, etc. The variations are generally ordered in progressive complexity. It is most useful to practice only a few variations per day but spend a good deal of time perfecting them. Doing too many exercises will be taxing to both the mind and muscles, and will not be very useful.

2
The Left Hand

While the right hand provides a beautiful tone along with various bow strokes, the left hand provides the ability to play a multitude of various pitches, including harmonics. Generally speaking, the technique of the left hand is much simpler than that of the right hand, though it requires even more work to maintain. Once the techniques required to play vibrato and perform shifts are developed, they must be practiced repeatedly in order to keep them in good form. In this chapter, I explain the fundamentals of the techniques used in each aspect of shifting and vibrato and provide several beneficial exercises to develop and maintain proficiency.

The most persistent problem the left hand faces is arguably intonation. In this chapter, I explain various methods and exercises to attain acceptable intonation, as well as provide analysis of, and suggestions for using, the three temperaments most used by violinists: Pythagorean, Just, and Equal.

Basics

Finger Pressure

The fingers must always press firmly into the string, but not so much as to prevent shifting. Pressing too much will cause tension and pain in the hand, while pressing too little will produce a weak tone or disgusting guttural sounds. This being said, great care should be taken to find the perfect amount of finger pressure needed to create a beautiful sound while keeping the hand tension-free.

Exercise

To determine just how much pressure is needed, play a piece of music slowly with the same pressure needed to produce harmonics (almost no pressure). Horrible sounds will be created, but the hand will be very loose and relaxed. Repeat the piece again, using slightly more finger pressure. The tone will probably be even more harsh and unappealing than the first time, but the hand will still be loose and relaxed. Repeat this exercise, using more and more pressure each time, until a beautiful tone can be created with the smallest amount of pressure being used.

While performing the above exercise, notice the different amounts of pressure needed on each string. Much less pressure is required to generate a beautiful tone on the E-String than the G-String. This being said, once a beautiful tone is achieved, do not increase the pressure on the upper strings just because more is needed on the lower strings. Also notice that more pressure is needed in higher positions than lower positions. This is due to the increased distance between the strings and fingerboard in higher positions. As with playing on different strings, do not use more overall pressure just because more pressure is needed in higher positions. Rather, vary finger pressure to suit the needs of each individual note.

When experimenting with finger pressure, many people make the mistake of neglecting finger agility. To ensure that the fingers remain fast and explosive, perform a piece of music slowly, forcing the fingers swiftly and determinately into the strings. Once the fingers depress the strings all the way into the fingerboard, release the pressure in the fingers so that the least amount of pressure possible is used.

Since using too much finger pressure can create tension and pain in the hand, take care to implement these exercises into the daily practice routine.

Elbow Position

The lateral position of the elbow can affect many aspects of violin playing, including intonation, shifting, vibrato, and others. Its position must be altered when various positions are used, as well as when different strings are used, in order to maintain a comfortable and healthy playing position, as well as pleasing intonation.

Elbow Position and Shifting

The position of the elbow changes quite drastically when playing in different positions on the violin. From first to fourth positions, the elbow remains mostly underneath the violin, supporting the hand. As the hand moves from lower positions to higher positions (5th – 8th positions), the elbow must move further to the right of the violin (toward the stomach) to allow the hand to move around and over the shoulder of the violin. When shifting back down to the lower positions, the elbow must move back underneath the violin.

When playing above eighth position, the elbow remains in front of the stomach, and the left hand handles the shifting motions on its own. Moving the elbow when in higher positions hampers the hand's ability to accurately perform tiny shifts.

Elbow Position and String Level

Just as playing on different strings requires different right hand levels, it also requires using different left elbow levels. Changing elbow position is essential to keeping that the fingers, palm, forearm, and elbow, are all in a straight line. If these parts of the arm and hand are not in a straight line, tension will develop, accuracy will be lost, and intonation will suffer. Furthermore, if this bad posture is allowed to take root, tendinitis may develop.

On lower strings, the elbow must move further under the violin toward the stomach in order to allow the fingers to reach all the notes comfortably. When moving to higher strings, the elbow should move to the left away from the stomach. Generally speaking, the elbow should form a right angle to the bow at all times. This being said, it will follow the seven different string levels in conjunction with the bow.

Vibrato

Vibrato is probably the most personalized aspect of violin technique and musicality. Since there are many ways to do vibrato on the violin, everyone's views and tastes are different. Throughout the Baroque (and earlier) Eras, vibrato use was very limited and often considered an ornament. As such, it was used rather sparingly. As a matter of fact, Leopold Mozart, a prominent musician, pedagogue, and theorist who lived towards the end of the Baroque Era, advocated against liberal vibrato use, stating: "Performers there are who tremble consistently on each note as if they had the palsy.[1]" Even violinists of the twentieth century felt that vibrato use should not be overdone. Leopold Auer, Heifetz's teacher, equated continuous vibrato use to over-seasoned food,[2] and even said that continuous vibrato was a "physical defect…[caused by] sick or ailing nerves.[3]"

Predictably, there were numerous proponents for vibrato, including Ivan Galamian, who stated that vibrato "Subliminally melds musical sounds with the deep feelings which subconsciously slumber in our souls.[4]" There were significantly more proponents for vibrato than opponents against it, and vibrato, even continuous vibrato, became commonplace during the Romantic and Modern Eras. During this time, notes were sustained longer which required the added warmth of vibrato. Soon, violinists became used to vibrating continuously, and vibrato use became so prevalent that violinists began using it unconsciously. This being said, I feel that artistic discretion should always be used when deciding which types of vibrato to use, and when. Continuous vibrato is nice, but vibrato speed and width need to be altered in order to prevent a boring monotonous tone.

There are two main types of vibrato: Arm Vibrato and Wrist Vibrato (also known as Hand Vibrato). They are produced quite differently and generate drastically-different tonal sensations. When first learning vibrato, it is often easiest to begin with wrist vibrato rather than arm vibrato. When beginning vibrato, the left hand is not usually loose and flexible. As such, it is necessary to build flexibility while teaching the muscles the vibrato motion.

The exercises provided in this section provide a solid foundation of flexibility and technique that can easily be enhanced through focused practice.

No matter which type of vibrato is used, the first joint of the finger that vibrates needs to be flexible. The amount of firmness or looseness in the first joint determines the speed and width of the vibrato. If a very slow and wide vibrato is desired, the second joint may be loosened significantly as well to allow for greater motion.

Always vibrate below the desired pitch, never above. This is very easy to accomplish if the rules suggestions provided in this section are followed. Though at times it may sound like vibrato occurs above the pitch, it actually only occurs below the pitch. If vibrato ever occurs above the pitch, the passage will sound out of tune and the listener will feel uncomfortable or on edge.

How to Begin Vibrato

Learning vibrato often seems like a daunting task that is filled with confusion, stress, failure, and only small increments of success. However, mastering vibrato can be quite easy, painless, and even fun. Complete the exercises in this section in chronological order for best results.

Exercise #1

-Place the third finger very lightly on the a-string, as if to play a harmonic. Using the same motion as is used in shifting, slide the entire hand from first position to the highest reachable note, and then slide back down.

-Perform this exercise very slowly at first. Once it can be performed effortlessly and tension-free, speed it up until the entire cycle from first position, up, and back to first position can be performed at 120 beats per minute.

-Perform this exercise with all fingers.

After completing this exercise, continue to the next section.

Wrist Vibrato

Wrist vibrato is created by an oscillation within the wrist joint that causes the joints of the fingers to expand and contract as the fingers roll from tip to pad, and back. Though either wrist or arm vibrato can be used to produce a vibrato of any speed or width, wrist vibrato tends to be most effective when a fast and narrow combination is used.

Exercise #2

- Place the hand in roughly 4th or 5th position so that the wrist is touching the rib of the violin and the thumb is in the crook of the neck. Place the first finger on the a-string. With a rocking wrist motion roll the first finger from its tip back onto its pad and back onto its tip.

- Complete this exercise with every finger on every string.

- When the student first begins this exercise, there may be very little change in pitch. As the student becomes accustomed to this exercise, the difference between the rounded finger and the flattened finger may be as large as a half-step.

- Once the student is able to perform this task adeptly, have the student do it in first position. Make sure the motion occurs only in the wrist. Do not let the forearm initiate the motion.

Exercise #3

Perform Exercise #2, but also make the base joint and second joint of each finger extend and contract. This exercise builds flexibility in the entire finger rather than just the first joint.

Exercise #4

- Place the third finger on the "F-Natural" in third position on the A-String.
- Like in the previous exercise roll the finger back onto its pad. However, when performing this exercise, release all pressure in the finger so that the E-Natural Harmonic sounds when the finger is rolled back onto its pad.
- Repeat this exercise with all fingers. Since natural

harmonics do not occur on every note, simply start on the same "F-Natural" as is played with third finger and release to the same "E-Natural" Harmonic.
- Repeat this exercise on the other strings in the same position.

Exercise #5

- Place the forearm, wrist, and hand flat against a wall.
- Using only the wrist, swing the hand away from the wall, and then back towards it. Tap the base knuckles against the wall when the hand swings back towards it.
- Make sure that the forearm stays stuck against the wall at all times. If it moves away from the wall, the wrong part of the arm will be performing the exercise. In this exercise, only the wrist moves the hand.

Use a metronome whenever possible when working on vibrato. Perform one cycle of vibrato per beat, gradually increasing the speed of the metronome until the vibrato is at an acceptable performance speed. Once vibrato can be performed well at an even pace using the metronome, play vibrato using the rhythms below.

Rhythm 1   Rhythm 2

Practicing vibrato with these rhythms will allow vibrato to be performed with even greater facility.

Arm Vibrato

Arm vibrato is created by an oscillation within the forearm that causes the joints of the fingers to expand and contract as the fingers roll from tip to pad, and back. When performing arm vibrato, it is important to keep the wrist immobile. If it is allowed to move with the arm, the wrist motion may cancel out the arm motion or even generate an uncontrolled, wild vibrato.

The ability to vibrate with the whole arm is a skill that every violinist should work to achieve at an early age. This type of vibrato tends to be slightly wider and slower than wrist vibrato, but can be sped up and narrowed rather easily. It is better suited for loud, intense passages than wrist vibrato, but can also create an unparalleled trembling effect in soft passages.

Continuous vibrato occurs when the vibrato effect is continuous from note to note. In other words, the vibrato never ends, even when notes change. This effect is easiest to achieve with an arm vibrato, as the arm can continue to move back and forth even when new fingers are used on the string. To achieve a continuous vibrato, simply keep the vibrato motion going while placing new fingers on the string. First practice continuous vibrato while playing scales. This is a great starting point, as adjacent fingers will be used for each new note. From here, practice alternating thirds, and then incorporate continuous vibrato in regular violin repertoire.

It is essential to artistically alter the speed and width of continuous vibrato to prevent a boring, monotonous, and nervous trembling sound from taking hold in the music. As the phrase grows and drops, the width and speed of vibrato should change accordingly.

Exercise #6

- Place the forearm, wrist, and hand flat against a wall.
- Using the entire forearm, swing the hand away from the wall, and then back towards it. Tap the base knuckles against the wall when the hand swings back towards it.
- Make sure that the forearm and wrist remain in a straight line. If the wrist moves separately from the forearm, the exercise will not be productive.

Exercise #7

When performing arm vibrato, beginners often shake the whole violin, or at least the scroll. To eliminate this habit, simply begin vibrating slowly and narrowly. Gradually increase the speed and width of the vibrato, always ensuring that the scroll and violin remain still.

Though it seems like switching between arm and wrist vibratos will create drastically different sounds, a violinist should be able to switch between arm and wrist vibratos without changing the sound. The primary way to change the sound of vibrato is by altering vibrato width and speed. These variables can be changed when using either arm or wrist vibrato, even though they are altered physically in different ways depending on which type of vibrato is used. In order to expertly craft the perfect vibrato for any given passage, it is necessary to alter vibrato speed and width individually. Vibrato can be used to create various effects or personalities in music. A slow wide vibrato can portray a sick old man, while a fast narrow vibrato can portray an overly excited kitten. While these two personalities are drastically different, they can easily be attained by altering vibrato speed and width.

Vibrato Width

Vibrato width alters the variability of pitch in vibrato. The wider the vibrato motion is, the more the pitch will change. Altering vibrato width provides the greatest variance in tone. If a *piano* sound is desired, the vibrato can be quick and narrow. This will produce a breathtaking trembling effect. If the tone changes from *piano* to *forte*, a different vibrato is required. The best vibrato for an enormously intense robust sound may be a quick wide vibrato. In both the *piano* and *forte* tones, the vibrato speed was constant (fast), but the width was altered. If the narrow speed was maintained while playing *forte*, the pitch would not vary enough and the sound would be untrained and boring.

Altering the width of vibrato is actually quite easy. To obtain a narrow vibrato, both the first and second knuckles of the fingers should be allowed to expand and contract very little. This will result in very little lateral motion of the fingertips. As such, very little tonal variance will occur. To obtain a wide vibrato, both the first and second knuckles of the fingers should be allowed to expand and contract as much as possible. This will result in a very large lateral motion of the fingertips. Predictably, a great deal of tonal variance will occur. The fingers should always be free from tension, no matter how wide the vibrato is. This being said, the fingers should be even looser when a wide vibrato is desired. This looseness will allow the greatest vibrato width possible.

When altering vibrato width, it is often advisable to alter speed to prevent a painful wailing vibrato tone. However, when experimenting with and working on vibrato, speed should stay constant when width is changed. When increasing vibrato width, students tend to slow down the vibrato. In many cases, students will have to think about speeding up vibrato in order to maintain a constant speed. This change in speed is very minimal and should not be exaggerated. Use a metronome to insure that speed does not increase or decrease when vibrato width changes.

Vibrato Speed

The ability to change vibrato speed is equally as important as the ability to change vibrato width. If a constant vibrato speed is used in all pieces and at all dynamic levels, the music will not be as emotionally riveting as possible. If a slow wide vibrato is used, the pitch will vary quite a lot. However, since the speed is very slow, the sound may be equitable to having indigestion. However, if the speed is increased, the resulting sound will be very intense and energetic. Rather than feeling ill, the listener may feel heroic. To alter vibrato speed, simply make the time it takes to complete one vibrato cycle shorter or longer. It is very useful to use a metronome when practicing vibrato speed. To practice altering vibrato speed, perform the following exercise:

Exercise

1. Starting with a slow metronome marking (Quarter Note = 60), perform two vibrato cycles in one beat.
2. Once this can be performed adeptly, perform three vibrato cycles in one beat.
3. Again, once this can be performed well, increase the number of cycles per beat to four.
4. Once this is performed effortlessly and steadily, the metronome marking can be increased incrementally (Quarter Note = 66; Quarter Note = 72, etc.).
- Repeat Steps 1–3 for each new metronome marking.

Shifting

Shifting is the motion that moves the hand from one position to another on the fingerboard. Though it requires a fair amount of practice to attain proficiency, the shifting motions are actually fairly easy to perform.

Essentials of Shifting

The hand must always be relaxed when shifting. If tension or pressure exists in any form, accuracy in shifting will be impossible. When shifting, the fingers must exert almost no finger pressure into the string.

"Phantom Finger" Shifts

When shifting between two positions, we must use "phantom" fingers. To play a phantom shift, the finger pressure must be almost completely relieved, as if playing a harmonic, and very little bow pressure and length should be used. Once the finger pressure is released, the hand moves slowly along the fingerboard. Once it reaches its destination, the finger pressure is again asserted into the string. During the shift, the pitch can be slightly heard. Use this as a guide for playing shifts in tune. In the following exercise, the phantom fingers are shown in blue.

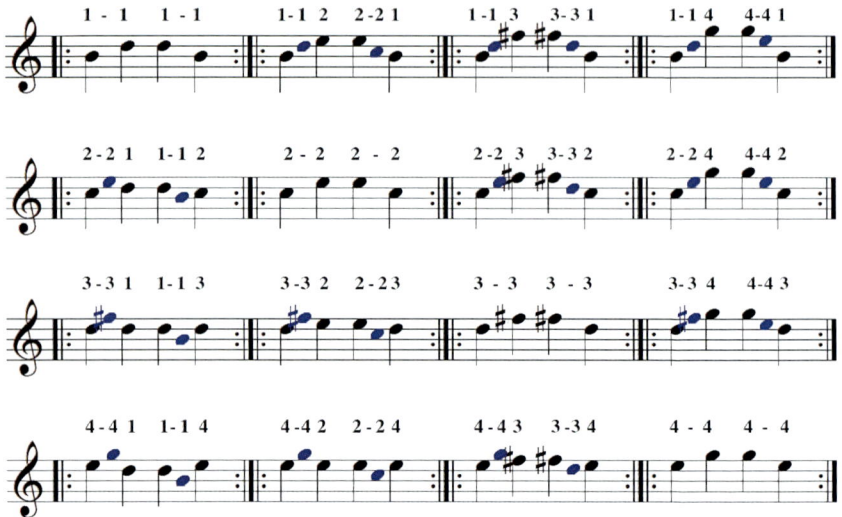

When shifting with phantom notes, the original finger performs the shift, moving from the old to new position. Once in the new position, the new finger is placed down. For example, if shifting from Second Finger C on the A-String in First position to Third Finger F on the A-String in Third Position, the second finger shifts from C to E, then the third finger drops to play F. To shift back to first position, the third finger shifts from F to D, and then lifts so that the second finger can play C. See how this is notated in the third measure of the second line of the above exercise.

It is important to note that the shifts in the above exercise are "Old Finger" shifts. To attain shifting proficiency, perform the exercise with both Old and New Finger Shifts on every string. This exercise can be adapted to go from any position to any other position (ex. From 3rd Position to 8th Position or from 1st Position to 5th Position).

Old Finger Shifts and New Finger Shifts

Old Finger Shifts, also called *French* or *Classical Shifts*, are the most common type of shifts used in music. As shown in the "Phantom Finger" shifting exercise above, Old Finger Shifts are performed by shifting on the original finger, then placing the new finger. After practicing these shifts diligently, it is possible to make the shift almost completely inaudible.

New Finger Shifts, also called *Russian* or *Romantic Shifts*, occur mainly in Romantic-Era repertoire. These shifts are performed by shifting on the new finger, rather than the old finger. As such, the new finger needs to be placed on the string before the shift occurs. Once the finger is on the string, the hand slides to the new position. Since the new finger is already on the string, no finger should be lifted once the new position is reached. See below for a "New Finger" version of the "Phantom Finger" shifting exercise. Unlike Old Finger Shifts, New Finger Shifts are usually played with a very noticeable glissando in order to add expression to the music. When using a shift to add expression to music, it is of the utmost importance to make sure that the hand does not shift so quickly as to upset intonation.

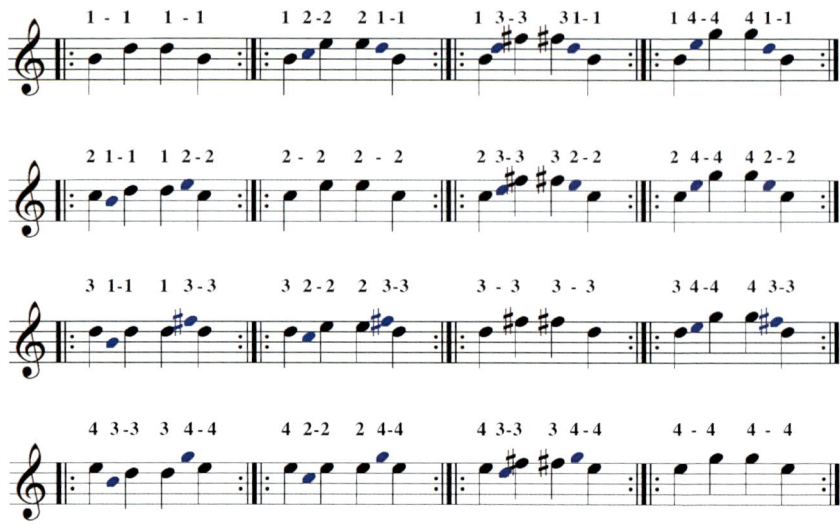

Elbow Movement While Shifting

The position of the elbow changes quite drastically when playing in different positions on the violin. From first to fourth positions, the elbow remains mostly underneath the violin, supporting the hand. As the hand moves from lower positions to higher positions (5th – 8th positions), the elbow must move further to the right of the violin (toward the stomach) to allow the hand to move around and over the shoulder of the violin. When shifting back down to the lower positions, the elbow must move back underneath the violin. When playing above eighth position, the elbow remains in front of the stomach, and the left hand handles the shifting motions on its own. Moving the elbow when in higher positions hampers the hand's ability to accurately perform tiny shifts.

Fast-Shift Exercise

Though the shifting motion must always remain slow and smooth, having the ability to perform swift, yet accurate, shifts is paramount. This ability is most useful in fast virtuosic passages, but also is incredibly useful in slower melodic passages. If shifts are too slow, the rhythm of the passage will suffer, intonation may not be as pleasant, and the violinist's sound will be immature. This exercise can be used to practice any shift on the violin. It can be used in both slow and fast passages.

Exercise

- Hold the beginning note of the shift for a few seconds.
- As quickly as possible, shift up to the second note of the shift and back to the first.
- Repeat this exercise an indefinite number of times until the shift can be performed accurately in as little as a millisecond.
- Always focus on intonation. Both the first and second notes should always be perfectly in tune.
- Take care to avoid "jumping" to the new note. The shift should still be smooth and controlled.
- Do not go too fast too soon. Speed cannot be attained without first going slowly.

Agility/Co-Ordination

I first heard the term "Co-Ordination" from violinist Susan Waterbury, my teacher at the Ithaca College School of Music. The term perfectly outlines the co-dependence and cooperation between the left and the right hands. In order to attain true proficiency on the violin, co-ordination between the two hands must be developed and practiced regularly. For most people, the left hand tends to lag behind the right hand, resulting in a diminished clarity of sound or even extra notes. There are several effective ways to correct this issue.

Fingers Before Bow

The easiest solution to this problem is to slow down and simply concentrate on having the fingers depress the string before the bow produces the sound. When first hearing this solution, it may seem like depressing the strings early would create the same problem, as one hand is moving before the other. However, moving the fingers before the bow actually remedies the issue, rather than exacerbate it. The following exercises help co-ordinate the hands by making the left hand move before the right hand.

Exercise #1

- Play an entire passage staccato or collé, including passages that are traditionally played legato.
- During the pause between notes, put down the next finger that will be used. This will ensure that the finger is not late.

- Only when the new finger is in place, play the next note. Repeat this process for every new note.

- Work on the passage very slowly at first. Only when the entire passage can be accurately and clearly performed should it be sped up. Do not go too fast too soon. Increase the speed very gradually.

Exercise #2

- Play an entire passage with a new, repetitious, simple rhythm. The following excerpt is from Kreutzer's Caprice No. 2. Notice how the notes appear in the various rhythms. Rhythms 1 and 2 are most useful when using a simple meter (two micro-beats per beat) and Rhythms 3 and 4 are most useful when playing a passage that uses a compound meter (three micro-beats per beat).

- When practicing a passage using these rhythms, be sure to practice multiple rhythms so that the rhythms simply remain an exercise, and do not take hold in regular performance.

Original

- In addition to helping the left hand attain proficiency, this exercise also provides an intense workout for the right hand. Take any passage of music and replace the traditional rhythms with short eighth, sixteenth, thirty-second, or sixty-fourth notes, depending on the tempo of the piece and what note values are in the original part.

- The notes that are played should still be of proportional length to one another. As such, if the smallest note value in a piece of music is a sixteenth note, keep that as the smallest note value. Replace all eighth notes with two sixteenth notes, all quarter notes with four sixteenth notes, all half notes with eight sixteenth notes, etc. If thirty-second notes are preferred, make the same proportional changes as described above.

- If playing a fast passage that already uses fast notes with the same note value, this exercise is still very useful. The bow will move much faster than normal, as even smaller note values than normal will be used. This will provide an intense workout for the right hand, as it will have to move quite quickly and efficiently.

- Sometimes, overlaying the smallest note value onto the entire piece is not as beneficial as overlaying a different note value. As such, overlaying eighth notes onto a movement is alright even if the smallest note value is a sixteenth note. When doing this, the sixteenth notes should stay sixteenth notes, rather than change to eighth notes. The following example overlays eighth notes onto the exposition of the First Movement of Mozart's Violin Concerto No. 5 in A Major, K. 219. The smallest note value is a sixteenth note. All sixteenth notes are performed as originally written.

- Start by holding the first note of the grouping much longer than normal.

- Proceed by playing the remaining notes in the grouping as quickly as possible.

- Repeat this for each new grouping of notes. Make sure that the same notes are sustained in each new grouping (always hold the first note, or always hold the third note).

- After the passage is clear, hold the second note in the grouping and rush the others. After this, hold the third note in the grouping and rush the others. Finally, hold the fourth note in the grouping and rush the others.

- The following passage is from Kreutzer's Caprice No. 2. Hold the fermata notes for longer than normal, and rush all notes that have a red arrow over them.

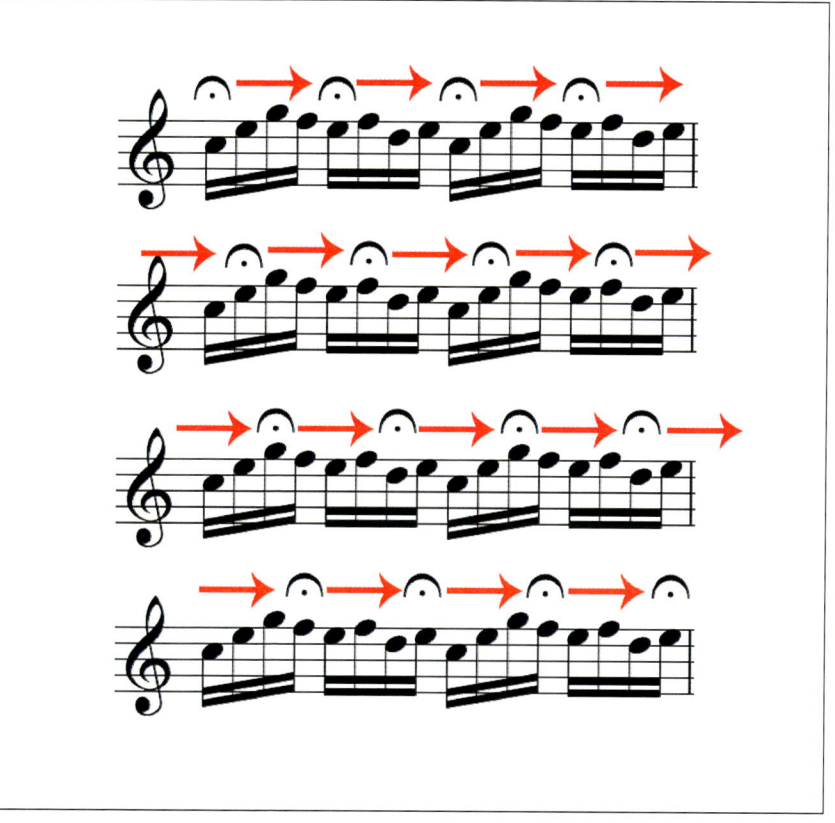

- This is by far my favorite exercise to help co-ordinate the hands in a fast passage. It trains the fingers to be able to play a passage very quickly, while remaining clear. While working on this exercise, notice which notes tend to slow you down. Repeat these sections until they are clear and accurate. This exercise can be applied to almost any passage of music that contains a series of notes of the same rhythmic value. If there are slurs in the original part, practice this exercise both with and without them for best results.

Independent Motion of the Fingers

The fingers should be trained to move independently from one another. This is no easy task, as the hand is predisposed to have the third and fourth fingers move together. In order for the fingers to gain freedom and independence, they must be strengthened. The following two exercises are from *The Violin Players' Daily Dozen: Twelve Fundamental Exercises for the Left Hand and the Bow, Op. 20* by Demetrius Constantine Dounis. These exercises work to strengthen the fingers while building independence. Begin working on these exercises slowly and gradually build up speed until they can be performed accurately at a swift pace. The fingers should always act as hammers, quickly and decisively depressing the strings. These exercises are performed without the bow. Repeat each measure dozens of times.

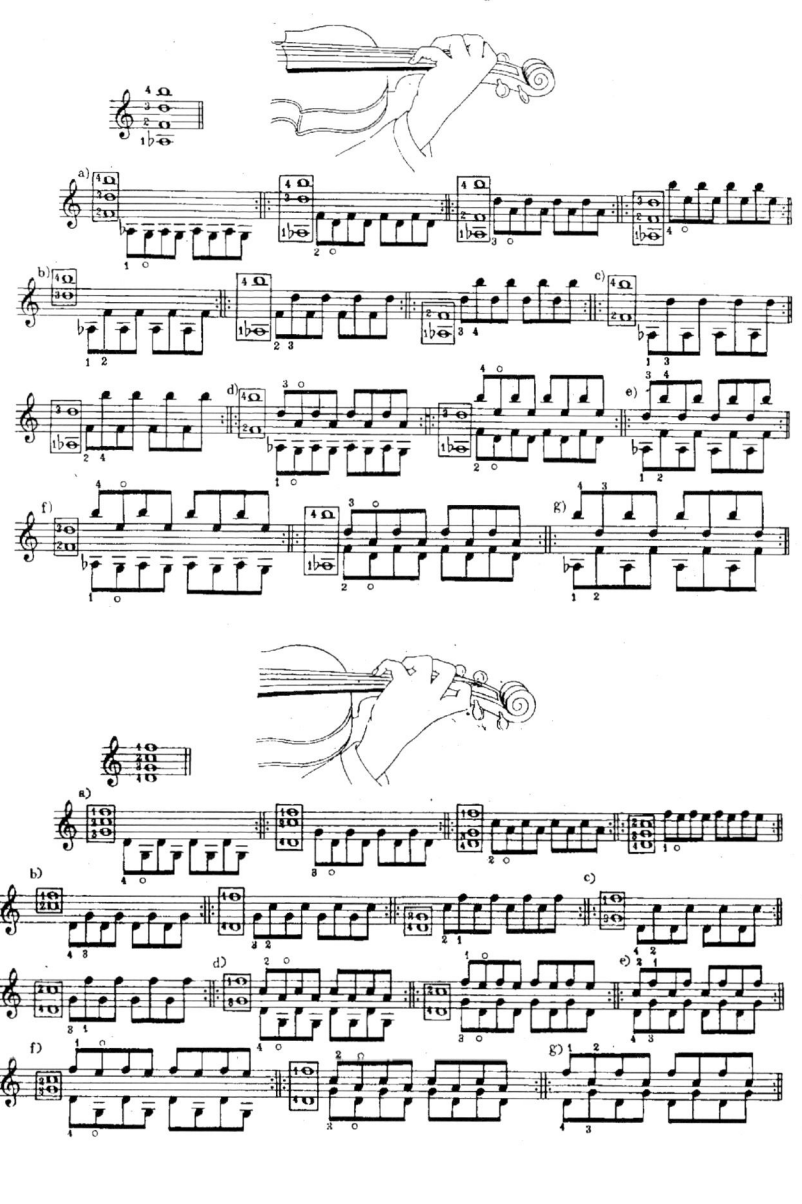

Intonation

Along with tone, intonation is one of the most important components of violin performance. Unlike the piano or guitar, the violin has no regulated tunings for notes, so we must constantly evaluate pitch and finger position and make adjustments as necessary. There are three main methods to use to tune a passage on the violin: Pythagorean, Just, and Equal. Each method creates an incredibly different character, and some methods simply sound better than others depending on the situation.

Pythagorean Temperament

Developed by Greek Philosopher and Mathematician, Pythagoras, this tuning has been used for thousands of years. This tuning revolves around the ratio 3:2, which represents the perfect fifth interval. To create a Pythagorean Tuning, start on C and perfectly tune an ascending fifth. Take the perfectly in-tune G that results and tune another ascending fifth above that. Repeat this process until you reach the next C.

Though this method of tuning seems perfect, as it uses the perfect fifth, it is actually quite flawed. The final C that is produced after going through the circle of fifths is incredibly out of tune, compared to the starting C. Predictably, many other notes are out of tune when tuning with this method. When playing a diatonic scale, scale degrees 3, 6, and 7 are sharper than in equal temperament. While this sounds just fine when playing a scale, it sounds incredibly out of tune when playing double stops or chords. When a keyboard instrument is tuned in this manner, not all notes are usable. For example, when playing an E Major Chord, the slightly sharp G-Sharp makes the chord sound more excited and joyous than normal. However, the A-Flat Chord (enharmonically equivalent to G-Sharp) is very out of tune, and is essentially unusable.

One famous instance of a Pythagorean tuning dilemma occurs just after the second entrance of the violin in the First Movement of Tchaikovsky's Violin Concerto in D Major, Op. 35 (shown below).

In this figure, the boxed notes show the tuning problem that occurs. We use Pythagorean Tuning to tune the violin strings, as they are tuned in perfect fifths. If the C is tuned to the low G, a wonderful perfect fourth interval is created. The E should traditionally be tuned to the E String so that the string resonates along with the covered note. However, when the double stop C-E is played with this tuning, it sounds discordant. This is due to the fact that E is the third scale degree in C Major, which is sharp in Pythagorean tuning. Rather than tuning E to the open string, it should be tuned flatter to sound in tune to the C. However, when this is done, the E is no longer in tune with the open string, as it is flatter than the open string. This being said, if the C is tuned higher, to sound in-tune to the open E String, it is no longer in-tune with the open G String that is played immediately after the double stop. There is no correct answer to this tuning question. Rather, the performer should experiment with this passage using different tuning methods until it finally sounds in-tune.

When to Use Pythagorean Temperament

Pythagorean Temperament works best when used in ascending melodic passages, a fact which explains why it is often called "Horizontal Tuning." Consecutive notes are tuned to each other, rather than being tuned to the chords to which they correspond. The sharp third, sixth, and seventh scale degrees in Pythagorean Tuning help provide forward motion to the passage, propelling the music to the cadence. This being said, Pythagorean Tuning should not frequently be used when playing in chamber ensembles, as the music will sound out of tune due to the various sharp scale degrees.

Just Temperament

Just Temperament is by far my favorite tuning method, as it always ensures that the underlying harmonic content of a piece will be in-tune. This harmonic intonation is very important in Early Music repertoire, of which I am quite fond. In this tuning method, the chords that correspond to the various scale degrees are always in-tune. This being said, when a diatonic scale is played, the third, sixth, and seventh scale degrees will be slightly flat. However, I personally feel that their flatness does not translate to poor intonation, but rather a slightly more mellow and round sound.

To achieve Just Temperament, adjust the two notes of a double stop until they sound in-tune with one another. Take care to only change one of the two notes at a time, as changing both notes will prevent you from understanding which note needs to be comparatively higher or lower in order for the double-stop to sound in-tune. In most cases, the lower note needs to be the guide note in the double-stop. It is placed in the proper position on the fingerboard from the start. The upper note is then altered to be in-tune to the lower one.

Just intonation is the preferred method of tuning in almost all chamber groups, as it produces beautiful sonorous harmonies. The exception is in groups that contain piano. This tuning consideration will be elaborated upon in the following section about Equal Temperament/Tuning. When playing solo Baroque repertoire that contains many double stops or chords, Just intonation should be used more frequently than Pythagorean Tuning. Though the intonation of the melody in any composition is of utmost importance, if the harmony is out of tune, the piece will lose its beauty and power. When playing a piece with chords or double stops, try to play using a combination of both Just and Pythagorean Temperaments. Use Pythagorean when only individual notes are played, but switch to Just intonation when chords are present. Always listen for intonation to ensure that the piece sounds in tune as intended.

Equal Temperament

The idea of Equal Temperament has been around almost as long as Pythagorean Temperament. One of its earliest advocates was Vincenzo Galilei, Galileo Galilei's father. In Equal Temperament, an octave is divided into twelve equal intervals. Each interval is one half step. Since each interval in the octave is equal, a piece will sound the same even if played in a different key. This tuning became very popular for keyboard instruments, as every harmony in a piece is usable. However, every piano will sound out of tune as a result of this tuning method. Since every interval is equal, the third, sixth, and seventh scale degrees will always be slightly flat. They are not as flat as in Just Intonation, but they are still too flat to be considered in-tune. This is the main reason why equal temperament, though being widely used by keyboardists, never really caught on with string players.

When to use Equal Temperament

As explained above, using Equal Temperament will result in any passage or chord sounding slightly out of tune. As such, it is very rarely used in string repertoire. However, when playing with a piano in either solo or chamber repertoire, using Equal Temperament may be appropriate in some places. This is due to the fact that the piano is tuned in Equal Temperament, and if the violin plays a passage in unison with the piano, it is better to match the piano's intonation, rather than play in-tune to oneself.

Choosing the Proper Tuning

A violinist should be familiar with each of these tunings, as they will all be used in violin repertoire at some point. As a general rule, chords and double stops should use Just Temperament, melodies should use Pythagorean Temperament, and passages played in unison with the piano should use Equal Temperament. No matter the situation, the ear is the final judge for all intonation cases. If a passage sounds out of tune, it must be fixed somehow. If a melody sounds out of tune when using Pythagorean Tuning, use a different tuning or alter any notes until they sound in-tune.

Double Stops and Chords

When playing two or more notes simultaneously, extra care must be taken to ensure that they are always in-tune to each other. As explained above, Just Temperament is more suitable than Pythagorean Temperament or Equal Temperament when playing multiple notes at the same time. Play all chordal passages using Just Temperament unless there is a better option for that individual passage. Double stops and chords should always be in tune to themselves.

Which Note to Adjust

Since double stops consist of two notes, we have two possible notes to change to make a passage in tune. There are two methods to changing intonation in double stops. In the first method, the bass note of the harmony always stays in tune to the other notes in the scale. By this, I mean that if a piece is in F Major, all F's will be identical, even if a "bVI" chord is played. Tuning this way ensures that the tonic is always preserved. However, if playing in a key that contains several flats, some notes, which normally resonate with open strings, will no longer resonate, as they are either too low or too high. The second way, my preferred method, consists of maintaining resonance by tuning the chords to the open strings whenever possible. Double stops which do not contain resonant notes are tuned, using Just Intonation, to the bass note of whichever chordal harmony is present at that moment.

When playing a series of double stops, always focus on the lower finger. The passage will be more in tune, as the hand frame is based on the lower finger. Also, the brain is better able to make adjustments if the bottom note is stationary and the upper note is allowed to be adjusted. If the higher note is stationary and the lower note is adjustable, the passage will most likely be out of tune, as the hand frame may become compromised.

Octaves

When playing octaves, it is of the utmost importance to think only of the first finger. Focus on both the intonation of the first finger and the shifting of the first finger from one position to another. Never focus on the fourth finger or try to shift with the fourth finger. The fourth finger is passive when playing octaves, and should never bake priority. It may be even more useful to play the lower note slightly louder than the upper note, as is done in an orchestral setting, to bolster the intonation of the note and provide support to the tone. When playing in high positions on any string, the fingering should change from 1 – 4 to 1 – 3 to allow for greater comfort and flexibility in the hand. When using this alternate fingering, still focus on the first finger.

Tenths

As in Octaves, the first finger should be the center of focus, and the fourth finger should be passive. This being said, playing with perfect intonation requires more attention when playing tenths than when playing octaves.

Reaching Backwards to play Tenths

When first learning Tenths, it is advisable to start on the fourth finger and reach back with the first finger to find the lower note, rather than to reach up to the fourth finger from the first finger.

Reaching up to find the fourth finger will almost always result in poor intonation, discomfort, and even injury.

To practice this backwards motion, place the hand into fifth position and play the F# – F# octave on the A – E Strings. Keeping the fourth finger planted into the fingerboard, stretch back the hand to reach D on the A String. The entire hand should rotate in a clockwise direction, and the base knuckles of the first and second fingers should move slightly towards the floor as the first finger reaches down towards the floor and back towards the scroll.

Once this motion is practiced extensively for many weeks (or even months in many cases), place the first finger on the lower note and then find the upper note by using the "reaching backwards" motion that was used previously. Once in position, take care to maintain the hand frame as to avoid unnecessary motion and discomfort caused by having to re-position the hand.

Natural Harmonics

Natural Harmonics are created by barely touching the finger to the string directly on one of the "nodes," or places where a harmonic is located. Technically, there are dozens of natural harmonics on each string, though only several of them are usable on the violin. On the G-String, the harmonics that are usable are: G, D, G, B, D, F-Natural, and G (in order from lowest to highest pitch). The A and B above the last G are also usable, but are difficult to maintain. The diagram below shows the pitches and easiest fingerings to use to attain the natural harmonic series.

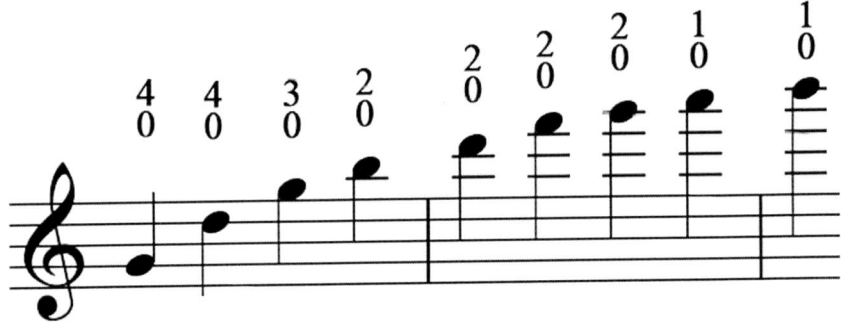

It is important to note that the harmonic series that exists on the violin is the same harmonic series that exists on brass instruments. When playing these harmonics, flatten the finger and play using the pad, rather than the tip. For most people, the finger will almost be completely straight. If the fingertip is used in place of the pad, the harmonics will be very difficult to find. Finally, it is important to mention that most harmonics are located slightly lower on the fingerboard than their notated pitch, if only slightly. This being said, if a regular note will be played on the same pitch as a harmonic on the same position on the string, the regular note is actually located slightly higher than the harmonic.

Artificial Harmonics

Artificial Harmonics are created by depressing the first finger into the string, as normal, and lightly touching the fourth finger to the string, as in Natural Harmonics. Since the first finger determines the pitch of the harmonic, an artificial harmonic can be played on any note on the violin. The diagram below shows typical artificial harmonic notation. The notes that sound are the lower pitches, but 2 octaves higher.

As in octaves and tenths, the first finger should be the center of focus, and the fourth finger should be passive when playing Artificial Harmonics. When working on a passage that contains Artificial Harmonics, start by playing octaves on the lower notes of the passage. This will train the hand to play the lower notes in the passage while maintaining a good hand frame. Only when the octaves can be performed in tune, should you move on to artificial harmonics.

Intonation Exercises

The following exercises can be used in almost any passage to aid in the perfection of intonation.

"Target Practice" Exercise

Part 1: Start by playing whichever note you would like to work on with a *mezzo forte* sound, focusing on intonation. Determine whether the note was placed too high, too low, or in the correct spot. Remove the left hand from the neck of the instrument and let it hang loosely at your side for about 10-20 seconds. Bring the hand back to the instrument and, without making any sound, place the finger back on the note. Play the note again and determine whether the finger placement is now too high, too low, or perfect. After repeating this process several times, one's tendencies will become obvious. Do not repeat this exercise without consciously trying to change finger placement. Repeating this exercise without changing finger placement is a waste of time, and also develops worse intonation.

Part 2: This exercise is also excellent for learning where each position is really located on the violin. This exercise can be used on any note, but as an example, we will use 1st finger B in fourth position on the E String. Perform Part 1 of this exercise until the note can be played reliably in tune every time. After you have mastered the exercise, repeat Part 1 using the second finger on the same note. Note: you will now be in third position, rather than fourth position. Again, practice this until it can be performed adeptly. Repeat Part 1 using third finger on the same note. You will now be in second position. Finally, repeat Part 1 using fourth finger on the same note. You will now be in first position. Once all four fingers can be performed in tune in their respective positions, repeat Part 1 but use a new finger and position each time the hand is brought back to the instrument.

"Imaginary Finger" Exercise

This exercise begins with our "imaginary" finger (second finger) being used. At the end of the exercise, it will no longer be used. This exercise can be adapted to any piece of music using any finger numbers. This exercise can even contain more than one imaginary finger. For example, if a piece of music uses first finger and then fourth finger, the second and third fingers can both act as imaginary fingers.

- To start, play the notes B, C#, and D in first position on the A-String. Take care to ensure that all fingers are played perfectly in tune. Once they are in tune, move on to the next step.
- Play first finger and stop. Put second finger into the string but don't play it. Rather, place third finger in the correct spot and play D. Once this is in tune, move on to the next step.
- Play first finger and stop. Do not put second finger on the string, but rather imagine that you are putting the finger into the string. You should feel the sensation in the finger of depressing the string, but do not actually let it move or touch the string. Place third finger in the correct spot and play D.
- Perform the previous step without the pause. Continue to feel the sensation of the imaginary second finger, but do not touch the finger to the string.

Compare to Next Note or Open String

This exercise is probably the most widely-used method for working on intonation in a piece of music. Start by playing the first note of the passage. If the note is in unison or an octave to an open string, match the pitch to the open string. If it forms a perfect fourth or fifth interval to an open string, tune the interval so that it is in tune. Once this note is in tune, play the next note in the passage. Unless the next note is in unison with an open string, an octave to an open string, or forms a perfect interval with an open string, tune the new note to the previous note. Tune notes to open strings whenever possible, as the open strings have standard tuning that does not change, considering the violin is in tune.

Using an Electric Tuner

I recommend using an electric tuner only for a drone. The drone can be set to almost any scale degree desired, as long as the musician understands that the tuner is set to Equal Temperament, and that every note the tuner plays will be slightly out of tune unless the pitch is raised or lowered accordingly by the player (if the tuner has that feature). I personally feel that the most useful note to play as a drone is the tonic (first scale degree) of whichever key you are in. Every other pitch that is used in a passage can be tuned to the tonic, even if the interval that is formed is as dissonant as a minor second or major seventh.

Pizzicato

Left Hand Pizzicato is a very useful technical tool for a violinist to possess. Not only can it be used for the special effect of playing pizzicato with the left hand, but it can also be used to provide clarity to runs or even slow melodic passages. To perform left hand pizzicato, move the elbow slightly further to the left (away from the stomach) than normal. Place the pad of the plucking finger to the left of the string and grab as much of the string as possible. The finger will be slightly flatter than normal, allowing more of the finger to grab the string.

Left hand pizzicato can be used to clarify runs, as well as beautiful melodic passages. To clarify runs, simply perform a pizzicato with each finger as you transition to the new note. The bow will move as normal. Since the string is plucked, an effect similar to a martlé stroke will be produced. By performing left hand pizzicato during runs, the runs will possess explosive clarity and brilliance. Oddly enough, pizzicato can also be used in slow melodious passages to make note changes even clearer than normal. Perform the pizzicato as if being used in a run, as described above. Next to the ear, the plucks will sound out of place and distasteful, but at a distance of only 15 – 20 feet, these little plucks will no longer be audible. The note changes will be very noticeable, but the smooth legato created by the right hand will be maintained.

Left Hand Technique, with all its nuances, is always a work in progress. Be sure to experiment with various combinations of vibrato until you determine what works best for a given passage. Since vibrato is different in various repertoires, try different combinations of speed and width until you find what works best. When practicing, devote at least 1 hour to various shifting exercises. While doing this, always concentrate on maintaining a clear and pleasing tone, perfect intonation, and most importantly, smooth shifts. Books like Otakar Ševčík's *Op. 8*, Gaylord Yost's *Exercises for Change of Position*, as well as most of Kreutzer and Rode Etudes and Caprices contain simple, yet musical, pieces that can be used to improve left-hand technique.

3
The Body and Mind

The various techniques of the left and right hands, which have been presented throughout the last two chapters, comprise only a portion of violin technique. The remainder comes from bringing together the body and mind in various ways to achieve comfort and equilibrium, avoid tension, allow the mind to delve deeply into the music, and become one with the instrument. Only when the body and mind work together can the violin become an extension of one's body.

This chapter discusses various aspects of posture and musical meditation. By breaking down the techniques required to become one with the instrument, the suggestions I offer not only improve the quality of a performance, but also promote an increased love of violin playing.

Stance

How a violinist stands not only determines how he or she looks when performing, but also greatly impacts the sound that individual is able to produce. Stance is physically influenced by the position of the feet, legs, torso, as well as psychologically influenced by the mind. In order to deliver the best performance possible, a violinist must understand how to develop and alter his or her stance. This is imperative to reach one's fullest potential as a musician.

Grounded Stance

Before beginning to play, try this visualization exercise to create a grounded stance. To begin, stand with your back straight and with your feet roughly shoulder-width apart and flat on the ground. Imagine that your feet, like trees, have long roots extending from them deep into the ground. These roots provide support and balance. Once the roots are firmly in place, focus on your knees. Allow all of the tension from the feet to the knees to flow down and out of the body. Next, visualize your thighs. Again, let all of the tension flow down and out of the body. Continue to release the tension from the rest of the body while focusing on the following body parts in order: feet, knees, thighs, buttocks, stomach, chest, shoulders, elbows, wrists, hands, fingertips, neck, cheeks, and forehead. Allow the entire body to relax. Try to maintain this tension-free stance and remain firmly rooted as you play your violin.

Balls of Feet

Now that you are able to play while feeling grounded, your stance must be slightly altered. Try this exercise: stand with your feet roughly shoulder-width apart and slightly shift your weight forward, onto the balls of the feet (towards your big toe – *not* the heel). Always ensure that the knees remain slightly bent to help support the added weight they need to carry. Your legs and torso will be roughly imitating the sensation of sitting on the very edge of a very high stool and leaning forward slightly. You should still feel grounded and remain firmly footed, as you practiced in the last exercise, but now you'll add a sensation of buoyancy and lightness. This slight flexibility and lightness comes mainly from the knees, though the feet can be allowed to move slightly further onto their tips and back down to the ground.

Stage Presence

Avoid unnecessary or distracting motions at all times. Stay connected to the music at all times, even when resting. Always stand with good posture and prepare your playing position slowly and deliberately.

Suspension/Lift

The sensation of buoyancy explained above exists not only in the legs, but also in the torso and armpits. This suspension will open up the body, creating added comfort and also creating more space in which to move around.

Exercise #1: Helium

While standing on the balls of the feet, imagine the sensation of having helium fill the chest cavity, slightly lifting the chest towards the sky. This suspension opens up the entire body and allows for arm weight to be fully released into the string without causing tension or constriction in the right arm.

In addition to the floating sensation you practiced in the last exercise, it is very beneficial to feel the sensation of the body being suspended from under the arms by bungee cords or huge rubber bands. Please note: the imaginary cords are not placed in the armpits, but rather between the elbow joint and the shoulder joint. The cords are not suspending the body completely, but rather gently elevating the arms. The arms should still fall in place naturally. The shoulders must always be relaxed and never elevated. If you notice that the shoulders are raised and it is difficult to relax when thinking of this suspension, do not continue to focus on suspension. Rather, move onto another exercise and come back to this one when the body allows.

This exercise will add buoyancy to the body and open up the arms and chest. There should always be space under each arm. The arms should always be up and away from the body, as to avoid tension and pain in the hands and arms. This being said, the arms should not be *lifted* by you from the side of the body, but rather *suspended* from the sky and allowed to hang naturally in the air with the fingerboard pointing towards the ceiling or parallel to the floor. This feeling of suspension not only relieves tension, but also promotes healthy shifting and vibrato techniques by providing the hand with enough room to perform the correct actions.

This type of suspension deals not with the body, but rather the mind. First, notice the f-holes of the violin. The openings are on the top of the violin, rather than on the bottom or on the sides. As you play, visualize the sound being sent upwards, rather than sideways. This is especially useful when playing chords or short notes. This upwards motion will add an unparalleled liveliness to the sound that will instill a sense of joy and energy that is otherwise unattainable. The psychological sensation of sending the sound upwards may also be matched by the right arm. At the end of strokes (not all strokes, but rather at the end of phrases or when the bow is already lifted), send the bow flying up towards the sky.

This physical upwards sensation experienced by the right hand can also be thought of as a rebound. At the end of a stroke, visualize a rubber-ball or basketball bouncing on the ground and bouncing high into the sky. This bouncy and buoyant sensation will allow the sound to really fly out of the instrument.

Relaxation

The body must be relaxed at all times. Any tension in the body will translate to some sort of restriction in playing. As such, it is paramount to work to attain true relaxation of the mind, body, and soul while playing violin.

Relaxing the Body

Before walking onto the stage, it is beneficial to sit in the Green Room, or dressing room, and completely relax the body so that the tensions of everyday life do not creep into the performance. Begin by sitting in a comfortable chair with feet roughly shoulder-width apart. The knees should be at roughly a ninety-degree angle and your feet flat on the floor. Do not lock the knees or allow them to bend more than ninety-degrees. Allow the hands to rest gently along the tops of thighs, with fingertips lightly touching just above the kneecaps. Concentrate on how the body naturally breathes. Don't try to regulate the breath, but simply breathe naturally and focus your attention on the breath. After a few minutes of mindful breathing, start to gain an awareness of tension within the body. Visualize these points of tension and inhale through them. As you exhale, visualize the tension flowing out of the body. Start by feeling the tension flow out of the fingertips. They should feel heavy and lifeless. Move on to the base knuckles of the fingers. Feel the tension flow out of them as they begin to feel heavy and lifeless. Continue to relieve tension by moving on, in order, to the palms, the wrist, the forearms, the elbows, the biceps, the shoulders, the chest, the stomach, the pelvis, the waist, the thighs, the knees, the remainder of the legs, the ankles, the tops of the feet, the arches of the feet, the base knuckles of the toes, and finally the tips of the toes. From here, move back up to the neck, then to the jaw, the cheeks, the ears, the eyes, the forehead, and finally the scalp. When complete serenity is achieved, sit for several minutes and enjoy the feeling of complete freedom from tension before moving on to the next section.

Relaxing the Mind and Soul

Maintaining the completely relaxed state from the last exercise, practice clearing your mind of all thoughts, whether good or bad. Any outside thoughts will corrupt the mind's ability to focus wholly on expressing emotion through music. There is no single process to relax the mind. Rather, everyone must determine what works best for him or herself. No matter what is done to achieve serenity, the emotions portrayed by the music must be explored in this deep, meditative state. When in this state, I personally focus wholeheartedly on the music I am about to perform. I carry myself through the plot of the piece, let my mind be engulfed by the various emotions I wish to portray, and remind myself of how I plan to carry the audience through the journey with me. After going through this process, I am usually immersed so deeply into the piece that I have no more space for outside thoughts. This serenity and emotional immersion should be maintained throughout the performance. Do not think of technique or anything else during the performance, but rather let the mind and spirit be swept up by the music.

Waking back up

Take time when emerging from the cocoon of serenity. Do not immediately jump back into activity, but move slowly. Start by becoming aware of your fingertips. They do not move, but rather attain the sensation of life. Continue to feel vitality in the rest of the body, following the same order of bodily focal points as when the body was relaxed. Once the entire body has regained its life, slowly open your eyes and begin slowly moving your fingers, then toes, then the rest of the body. Slowly come to your feet. Keep your mind focused on the emotions you plan to portray to your audience through your music as you slowly, but deliberately, walk to the stage.

Tips for Musicality

Programmatic vs. Absolute Music

Some pieces of music were composed with a specific story in mind. These compositions are considered "programmatic music." These pieces have a pre-determined emotional and musical journey, which, though slightly adjustable and adaptable, should be maintained by the performer. This being said, many pieces were composed without a plot, but rather with the intention of providing simple enjoyment. These compositions are considered "absolute music." When performing this type of piece, it may be incredibly useful to write your own plot. Setting a story to a piece of music gives the performer true ownership of the work and allows the performer to connect with it on an even deeper level than is possible otherwise. The story can be about anything from finding love to experiencing the different flavors of a meal. No matter the subject, it is important to have something in mind when playing.

Play For the Audience

Far too often, musicians perform for the sake of performing or to impress the audience. Not only are these not reasons to perform, but if a performer tries to impress the audience or perform for no reason, the performance will not be musical, and will actually not impress the audience at all. A performer should always play with the intention of giving the audience a way to enter the emotional world that you create and experience the musical journey with you. That being said, you should always play with the audience's enjoyment at heart. They can tell when you are playing for the sake of playing or if you are trying to impress them, and they will not enjoy the performance as much as if you are playing with their enjoyment in mind.

Jokes

Music has always been a source of enjoyment and humor. Even musicians like Haydn, Mozart, and Ysaÿe used humor in their compositions to create a more playful, amusing, and enjoyable performance. Though pieces are not always humorous, it is fun for both the performer and the audience if small bits of humor are present. Humor can be created by adding witty pauses, unexpected dynamic changes, changing bow strokes, varying the way music is played during repeats, or even making comedic facial gestures.

Improvisation

Though most pieces of music do not warrant improvisation in the traditional sense of the term, all pieces should be played as if they are being made up. This will ensure that every performance will fresh, spontaneous, thoughtful, and unexpected. I like to vary my performances so that I bring something new to the audience each time I perform. Though the perception of spontaneity is the goal, I always have a general idea of what I will do before I walk on stage. I always try to keep the fingerings and bowings the same each time I perform to ensure proper intonation and a pleasing tone.

The various techniques of the left and right hands, when compartmentalized, generate neither the most proficient technique, nor the most effective and beautiful musicality. As explained in this chapter, the body and mind unify violin technique. Only when the entire body works in unison can harmony, both physical and tonal, be attained.

Notes

1. Mozart: *A Treatise on the Fundamental Principles of Violin Playing.*

2. Auer: *Violin Playing as I Teach it.*

3. Auer: *Violin Playing as I Teach it.*

4. Galamian: *Principles of Violin Playing and Teaching*

Selected Bibliography

Auer, Leopold. *Violin Playing as I Teach it.* New York: Frederick A. Stokes Company, 1921. Print.

Fischer, Simon. *Basics: 300 Exercises and Practice Routines for the Violin.* London: Peters Edition Limited, 2011. Print.

Flesch, Carl. *The Art of Violin Playing.* New York: Carl Fischer, 2010. Print.

Galamian, Ivan. *Principles of Violin Playing and Teaching.* 2nd ed. Englewood Cliffs, N.J.: Prentice-Hall, 1985. Print.

Mozart, Leopold, and Edith Knocker. *A Treatise on the Fundamental Principles of Violin Playing.* Oxford: Oxford UP, 1985. Prin

About the Author

Author of the works: "Playing the Violin: A Pedagogical Analysis of Violin Technique and Performance Practice," and the Comprehensive String Series: "Early Success," Derek Voigt is an internationally acclaimed violinist and pedagogue. He is currently the Director of the String Music Department at Chatfield College near Cincinnati, Ohio. An experienced performer, Derek performs frequently in solo recitals, including performances in Paris, France, Alba, Italy, a unique solo experience with an Italian Chamber Orchestra sponsored by the UN and the Italian Consulate in New York City, and performances in several other locations in the US.

Derek has performed in masterclasses with Christopher Hogwood, Charles Castleman, Elmar Oliveira, and Janet Sung. He began his violin studies at age 3, studying with Dmitry Gerikh. He studied Violin Performance at the Ithaca College School of Music with Susan Waterbury, and at the University of Cincinnati College-Conservatory of Music (CCM) with Dr. Piotr Milewski. When not performing solo repertoire, Derek can be found performing chamber and orchestral repertoire.

Derek has performed with professional orchestras and opera companies such as the Buffalo Philharmonic Orchestra, the Orchestra of the Southern Finger Lakes, the Northern Tier Symphony Orchestra, where he served as the orchestra's Concertmaster, and the Cincinnati Chamber Opera, where he served as Principal Second Violin. Derek has served as concertmaster for numerous other ensembles, including the Grassroots Festival Chamber Orchestra in Ithaca, New York, the Voices Multi-Cultural Chorus' Orchestra, and the New Violin Family Orchestra.

An Early Music enthusiast, Derek has played Baroque Violin in Cornell University's Early Music Ensemble, Les Petits Violons. In this ensemble, he worked closely with great musicians like Neal Zaslaw and Christopher Hogwood. He currently owns an unconverted violin made in the early 1700's. Derek is also interested in 'new' instruments. He has played Soprano Violin in the New Violin Family Orchestra. This instrument is smaller than a typical Violin and is tuned a fourth higher (C-G-D-A). It can be thought of as an octave above a viola. It produces a very unique sound and allows for some very high notes. Derek also owns a unique Piccolo Violin. This instrument is tuned an octave higher a traditional violin (G-D-A-E). This instrument can be used to perform traditional violin repertoire at a very high pitch.

In 2010, Derek became the Founding Executive Director of the Tompkins County Youth Orchestra in Ithaca, NY. Since Derek's departure from Ithaca, the group has changed to become the Ithaca Youth Orchestra.

In 2008, Derek founded the 501-(c)(3) Non-Profit Organization, The Violin Player. The organization advances music education by providing quality musical instruments, as well as other educational resources, to schools and individuals in Ohio and New York. Please see: www.TheViolinPlayer.org for more information.